Praise for *Laughing Through the Tears*

"In this powerful and inspirational book, we come to understand the power of leadership, imagination, and family values and how they come together. Absent of sentiment or despair, CEO Luther Nussbaum takes you on his personal odyssey and thereby illuminates the connection between leadership and work-life balance with astounding force."

Warren Bennis, noted author
and lecturer on leadership

"You and Gin experienced every parents nightmare and you became a model for how every parent should approach every parenting responsibility . . . with passion and purpose and unconditional love. You clearly were brilliant . . . . You too, experienced the growth that occurs out of adversity and shared it in the most amazing and personal way in your book."

Tammie McMann Brailsford, COO of
the Aquarium of the Pacific, nurse and
former hospital administrator

"This is an exceptional work . . . . It is a book that needs to be available to encourage those who face the ultimate test of one's faith to believe and press on."

Martin P. Levin, prominent industry
insider, former publishing executive and
literary lawyer

[handwritten dedication, partially legible:] Dear — thanks for being so committed to your patients — their journeys — be as successful — Karis. To Nhut January 15, 2007

LAUGHING THROUGH THE TEARS

A Father/Daughter Love Story of Death and Recovery

Luther Nussbaum

KayT Publishing
Long Beach, California

First printing 2002

ISBN 0-9716565-0-9
LCCN 2001099269

TABLE OF CONTENTS

To Kristin
the almost forgotten daughter

PROLOGUE

The plane banked, giving us a view of the relatively virgin sands of Playa Palmar in Ixtapa. A brand-new resort had been hacked out of the jungle not far from the old coastal fishing village of Zhuatanello. My parents leaned forward from the seats behind us. Mom said, "Is Kari awake yet?" Kari was our eighteen-month-old. Her thumb and blue "blankie" gave her plenty of comfort to be fast asleep anywhere, anytime.

Through interminable customs and a harrowing taxi ride, we could only think about our mind's snapshot of the pristine white beach. Remembering our own first view of the Pacific, we were excited about going to the ocean for the first time with our new daughter. It was a bonus to share the experience with my parents. The front desk extracted our name, rank, and passport number. Then we were ceremoniously guided to our rooms by the staff of the second hotel on the beach. From there, we were focused only on getting to the ocean and getting into the water.

We changed Kari into her tiny powder-blue-with-white-trim bathing suit. My dad and I each took one of Kari's hands as we went over the crest in the sand and walked down to the water's edge. Kari looked out to sea and then down to the froth that was tickling her toes. As boldly as Magellan, she proclaimed, "My ocean!"

* * * * *

It was September when our three-year-old walked hand-in-hand with her parents toward the red barracks that served as the Montessori school in Columbus, Indiana. Our brave, precocious daughter was hesitating. Finally, after a tearful parting, Kari followed her new teacher, Mr. Dunnick, into the classroom. He turned to her and said, "Carrie, let me introduce you to some of your classmates."

She responded as a correcting teacher, "My name is Kari, not Carrie. That's car, beep-beep, eeeee."

* * * * *

I was in the office when the call came. I had standing instructions that any member of my family could interrupt me at the office. My wife was on the line. "Lu, Kari is sobbing uncontrollably. I don't know what's wrong. I need your help. Something happened at school."

I excused the associates who were with me in the office and turned back to the phone. "Gin, let me talk with her." Gin handed the phone to our nine-year-old daughter. I could understand little through the sobs and gasps. Finally, I said, "Kari, settle down. Tell me what's wrong."

"Dad, I got a B on a test. I won't be able to get into Stanford." Until that moment I did not appreciate how much my first-born daughter was trying to emulate me and to please me. We truly had a special relationship.

CHAPTER ONE

A Turn in the Road

The sun was hanging mid-sky through the remaining veil of coastal fog. I stepped out onto grass that was still wet from the morning sprinklers and as I began to stretch, I took a long, deep breath. The air was incredibly still and heavy. I was in the habit of running about five miles four to five times a week; but after the chaotic events that had taken place just a few hours before, I was lucky to have even made it home. I was exhausted.

As I sat there stretching on the moist lawn, I looked out at the street. It seemed endless. There was pavement as far as the eye could see from ground level. *Who am I kidding, I don't have the strength for this*, I thought to myself. Truthfully, I shouldn't have tried to run that morning. Maybe I figured it would be a cathartic experience. There were tides of emotion churning inside me and I needed to sweat them out. So against my better instincts I decided to run.

By noon I was underway. I felt terrific as I rounded the first corner onto Highridge, so I quickened my pace a bit. I converted all of my pent-up feelings into raw energy. I was flying.

Then, about a mile into my run as I turned up the first moderate incline, I felt a wave of anxiety pass through me. Seconds later another one followed. This terrifying force quickly began to drain the strength from my body. Movement became laborious. I was in great aerobic condition, but for some reason I was gasping for air. My body was in severe pain. *I have to stop running,* I thought. Whatever had been festering deep inside of me over the past twenty-four hours had finally risen to the surface. It was crippling.

Exhausted, I collapsed onto the curb to catch my breath. I looked out over the surrounding houses, down toward the ocean, and tried to let the morning stillness calm my nerves. Gradually my strength began to return. Meanwhile, my mind began to draw me back into the events of the night before. Once again I was engulfed by the tragedy that had forever turned my world upside-down.

* * * * *

It was April 2, 1993, about 10:00 P.M. and I was already getting ready for bed. My wife Ginger was cleaning up downstairs and our younger daughter Kristin was in her room with a friend who was sleeping over. Kari, our soon-to-be eighteen-year-old, had gone out to a party. I heard a low rumble coming up from the street. The noise got progressively louder until shadows were arching over the walls and ceiling, flickering from one end of the room to the other.

Is Kari home already? I asked myself, vaguely puzzled. I listened for her to come in. Instead there was a loud knock on the door.

Kristin was the first to notice that a sheriff's deputy was paying us a visit. "Kari got busted by the cops!" she yelled excitedly to her friend Kendra.

I heard Gin answer the door. "This is *just* what I need," I muttered, pulling my pants back on. As I stepped out onto the upstairs balcony, I heard the officer's quiet words: "Your daughter's been in an accident. She's been taken to Harbor-UCLA. Would you like to follow us?"

I rushed downstairs. Every parent's worst nightmare had suddenly become a reality for me. I found myself fighting a burst of frustration. Why would Kari endanger herself during such a critical part of her life? *It's one thing to run away to a friend's house for a few days,* I thought. *But an accident is going to mess up her graduation.* I was truly upset by that prospect. I had no comprehension that my worst fears at that moment should have been my fondest hopes.

As I arrived at the front door, I asked the officer, "What shape's she in? What's broken?"

His expression was a study in detachment. "Sorry, sir. All that I can tell you is that she's been in an accident and that we need to go. *Now.*"

I stared at him in utter disbelief. *This can't really be happening. Hasn't my life been bad enough lately? Now my night is screwed.* Of course I wasn't thinking clearly, letting my selfishness get the best of me. But that's the way I was feeling during that difficult period of time. I took a deep breath, ran upstairs, and finished dressing. I threw on a long-sleeved cotton pullover and quickly shoved my feet into my shoes.

We walked into the garage and got into the car. Nobody said a word. We were confused and shaken up, silenced by dread. In retrospect, I probably should have been petrified. Instead, I was concerned, upset, and pissed off. I was in no way prepared to face the fact that Kari could be seriously, even fatally, injured. I was completely out of touch with reality. By the time we had pulled out of the garage the police car was gone. I began driving down the street but I wasn't really even functioning.

The accident was on Crestridge Street, less than a mile from our house. We arrived in less than two minutes to find that a police barricade had blocked off the entire street. I stopped the car, preparing to get out and walk a half block down to the scene. Gin tried to bring me out of my stupor, "Lu, what are you doing?"

"I'm pulling over so that we can go see—"

"No, you're not. Drive over there to the right, around the barricade!"

I carefully maneuvered the car through the obstacles as if I were in driver's ed. Gin was beside herself, "Hurry up, Lu! For God's sake, Kari needs us. *Now! Please…let's go!*"

I could barely hear her. All of the sights and sounds around bled together. Sensory overload stifled my wits.

When we got past the barricade, I vaguely noticed that our deep blue Previa van was on the shoulder, off the left side of the street. I don't recall seeing much of it. All I can remember is noticing Kari's friends Laurie Scribe and Jessica Burtis, sitting on the curb on the right side of the street. We were so numb, Kristin had to remind us that we should pick them up. Gin jumped out of the car.

*They must have been with her…*I thought, feeling suddenly relieved to see that they weren't hurt. I felt a flicker of encouragement. *Maybe Kari's not in such bad shape after all*, I told myself.

The girls unsteadily climbed into the car and I began to drive toward the hospital again. Gin turned to the back of the car, "Are you two all right?" she asked.

The girls were both staring at the floor. Jessica was trembling. Eventually Laurie looked up and said feebly, "Yeah. We're…okay. Just a few bruises."

"What happened back there?"

The girls looked at each other, and finally Laurie spoke, "We went to one party for a while but it got lame pretty fast, so we left to go look for another one. We were driving down Crestridge trying to, like, meet up with some of our friends so we could look for another party together. We pulled off to the side of the road to wait for them. Then they came up the hill on the other side of the road and flashed their lights at us. Kari made a U-turn so we could follow them…" Laurie again began to stare at the floor.

"Kari made a U-turn and then what?"

Laurie looked out the window. Her eyes were glistening.

Gin was persistent. "I know this is really difficult for you and…but we really need to know what happened."

Jessica continued where Laurie had left off, "So Kari made a U-turn and as we were turning, we all saw an Explorer coming right at us. Kari said, 'Oh shit,' and hit the brakes. Then she tried to get away but it was too late. She was driving with her left foot up on the dashboard like she always does and the other car smashed right into her side, into her door, and…"

There was a long pause. "They had to use the Jaws of Life," Laurie's voice suddenly broke, "to get Kari out of the car."

"Oh my God!" Gin turned toward me, but my mind was elsewhere. *This is Vermont Street. I have to turn left here.*

"Who was in that other car?"

"Five sophomores," Jessica said faintly. "They had just left a party, too, and they came over the top of the hill. The driver, Gregg Hall, had, like, just gotten his license. He told some people after the accident he was afraid to brake too hard because he thought he might roll his car."

I heard the words and I stored some of them, but I couldn't really assimilate anything that was being said. *The hospital's down this way, somewhere on the left.* I had never been to Harbor-UCLA. Most of our friends' hospitalizations had taken them to Torrance Memorial or Little Company of St. Mary.

I do remember that at some point during that endless drive, Laurie told us she'd held Kari's head in her hands from the backseat until the ambulance got there. Gin flinched noticeably as though the real impact of what had happened finally sunk in.

This sudden bombardment of horrific information sent me deeper into shock. On a good day, I couldn't have intellectually processed and emoted over this event. But that night I was utterly overwhelmed. I remember once seeing on a talk show an individual whose parachute had failed to open when he jumped from an airplane. The talk show host asked him how he felt when he hit the ground. The individual said it felt no different from someone hitting him with a pillow. The sensory overload from thousands of screaming nerve cells must have been blocked as the signals flooded his brain.

I guess I was in a similar situation that night. With my mind reeling from shock and my ears trying to listen to everything the girls had to say, my thoughts focused on getting to the hospital. I was overloaded. I slowed the car to well below the speed limit. I couldn't even process driving at 30 miles an hour.

Gin was about to come out of her skin in frustration. "Dammit, Lu, you're driving like we're in a traffic jam!"

"Gin, if I drive any faster we'll have another six people in the ER. We're almost there. Cool it, dammit." As much as I truly meant to keep everyone calm, I knew that it was impossible. A deep, unfamiliar fear was eating away at me. My emotional core heard more than my brain accepted. My body knew it was going to be bad, really bad. My brain refused to process that thought.

The police officer had told us Kari had been taken to the Harbor-UCLA trauma center. It offered the best possible treatment, but it was 10 miles from our Rancho Palos Verdes home, and we had to pass two other, more familiar hospitals. When we finally got there, I dropped Gin and the girls off at the emergency room door and started looking for a parking place. The situation felt eerie and unreal to me. I was driving around and around the parking lot, knowing Kari was terribly hurt somewhere inside the building and being unable to reach her.

It took me five or ten minutes just to find a place to park the car.

At last I walked into the ER, reflecting on the strangeness of the day. *Of all times for this to happen*, I thought. I had been feeling depressed all day. The fact was, at that point in my life, things were not coming together the way I'd have liked them to. For one thing Kari, who had always been so incredibly special to me, was pushing away. Like nearly every other teenager, her life was undergoing drastic changes in a very short period of time.

In a matter of weeks, Kari would be graduating from high school. Afterward, she was facing the uncertainty of not knowing where she would be attending college. She had been rejected by her first choice, Emory University. She was happy about the prospect of going to one of her back-up schools, the University of Colorado at Boulder, but she was still waiting to hear from Lafayette and Lehigh. In the meantime, Kari was an adult now—she had made that clear in no uncertain terms—and she wasn't sure just what she wanted to do. She felt she needed to spread her wings and break free from our parental control. I knew she was struggling. I knew she needed my support and encouragement. But I was so wrapped up in myself and my own problems I'd failed to give her the kind of attention she should have had.

In the fall of 1992, I had left my job with Evernet Systems. Evernet was a venture capital startup, funded by the premier firm, Kleiner Perkins. It had been founded and made its first acquisition when I was brought in as CEO. After my coming on board, we had acquired like mad, inking thirteen deals in less than three and a half years. The regional units had been profitable, but barely so. We had believed and then believed some more that in only a few more months our profitability would offset the corporate expenses. We were sure that if we were given just a little longer, Evernet would be running in the black.

Eventually, we soared from a startup to more than $50 million in revenues. We raised more than $20 million in venture capital in pursuit of a great concept, or so we thought. Then, in the summer of 1992, it became clear that to raise one more round of funds to bridge us to be sold, I needed to step down. I was an impediment in two ways. I was putting too much pressure on the people within the organization while I was trying to will our success. I'd had good intentions, but my constant pressure on people sure must have made them feel otherwise. The second impediment was my unshakable belief that the business was close to success. I didn't want to change the business in major ways in order to dress it up for sale. Sometimes, it is just time to leave; that had been my time.

Now the day of Kari's accident had found me struggling with uncertainty, not knowing where my next job would be. I was talented and bright, yes. But I was still unemployed and getting more restless by the day. Still, ever the optimist, I had convinced myself the pain Ginger and I were both experiencing would soon be over once I accepted a new job and Kari decided where she was going to school.

Gin and I had gone to a movie that evening to pick us up. Even that had been depressing—it turned out to be a dark comedy and it had brought me down even more. At some level it stirred up my worst insecurities about parenting in particular and about life in general.

With disturbing thoughts still conflicting between emotion and logic, I hurried into the emergency room and immediately found myself surrounded by a mass of humanity. *I just can't believe this happened today*, I thought to myself. *Why did this have to happen to me?* I started thinking about all the other times we had taken the kids to the emergency room

and had to wait for hours to get them admitted. I was instantly annoyed with the hospital, assuming Kari's admission
was going to take far too long. *Why can't hospitals learn to run
emergency rooms right?*

I really wanted to feel sorry for myself that night. Fortunately I didn't have the time. Far more pressing problems
would soon require my full attention.

My eyes scanned the crowded room. Where was Gin? I
felt a surge of panic. *How am I going to find her?* All at once I
desperately needed her. I presumed she had gone with Kari to
admitting. I walked around aimlessly, growing angrier with
each step. *Why didn't she leave one of the kids in the waiting
room to give me directions?* Finally after a few minutes, Gin
appeared. She was sobbing, trying unsuccessfully to control
herself.

"Lu," she murmured, "it's really bad."

"Is she...alive?" I was frozen in place, with fear clutching
at my throat.

Gin nodded her head but she couldn't speak. Just then a
doctor hurried over to us.

"Mr. and Mrs. Nussbaum, could you come with me for a
moment?" Already scrubbed, he led us into a tiny conference
room. "I'm Doctor Holland, a fifth year resident," he explained, "and I'm going to begin the preliminary procedures
while the chief of surgery is en route." His tone was extremely
somber. "Your daughter has suffered a severe head trauma.
We ran a CAT scan on her and detected a large subdural
hematoma on the left side of her brain."

"Just exactly what does that mean?" my voice sounded
sharper than I intended.

"Essentially it's a blood clot resulting from the severe blow
to her head. Since there's so much blood in the area, we
weren't able to see if there was any damage behind the clot."
His voice was a monotone, probably intended to mask any

emotions he may have been feeling. "We suspect the brain has sustained significant damage, but we won't know until we've completed the procedure. We'll also have to operate on her left leg, which is fractured, and she has a pelvic bone that is broken in two places. Since she is unconscious and not moving at all, we don't need to do anything about the pelvic bone. We also need to take a look for any internal injuries."

I felt as if I had received a violent body blow and was trying to fight back the tears. Gin crumpled into a chair. Looking back, I don't know how I could have possibly thought Kari was going to make it through the night. Gin heard she might not make it. Yet somehow, drawing from some deep reservoir of hope or denial, I was already moving my thoughts forward, toward the moment we would all be together again.

The doctor rose and excused himself. "I need to get to work. There's a waiting room up on the second floor. It's just to the right, when you get out of the elevator. You and your family can stay there tonight."

"Thank you and..." I took a deep breath, "please take care of my daughter."

"All I can say is that you'll need to be patient," said the doctor. "It's going to be a long night."

CHAPTER TWO

Sè Rompio

The waiting room was deadly ugly, with overhead lights that were far too bright. Bolted to the floor, a dozen orange plastic seats couldn't even be moved, much less arranged comfortably. A flickering TV droned on with the dullest of nighttime fare. I looked at it blankly and saw moving images, but I didn't hear, nor care to hear, what they were saying. Gin, Kristin, Kendra, Kari's two friends, and I sat in silence for an eternity, wondering, waiting, worrying. At some point I glanced at the clock, assuming we were getting close to the time when we would be given a report about Kari, when we could go and see her. No more than five minutes had passed. Time seemed to be suspended.

I kicked off my shoes and shifted again in my seat. Dr. Holland hadn't said anything about the length of Kari's recovery. *It's going to be a tough couple of days, watching her try to recover from the brain surgery,* I told myself. I recalled a Harrison Ford movie that I had seen recently, which had told the story of a similar event. Ford's character had been shot, but later on he had suddenly recovered. *Kari can make that kind of a recovery. She's a fighter. If anybody can do it, she can.*

Hope battled against despair; optimism warred with the cold, hard facts. It wasn't long before I resigned myself to the reality that I wasn't going to get any sleep in those plastic bucket chairs. All of my life I've been able to sleep sitting up, but those chairs were exceptionally inhospitable. They provided no support above the lower third of my back. It was impossible to get comfortable.

Desperate to escape from the endless wait, I slid out of my seat and curled up my weary body in a fetal position on the cold linoleum floor. I shielded my eyes from the blinding hospital lights. Unexpectedly, like a slide show, memories of Kari's life began to flash through my mind.

* * * * *

On April 5, 1975, I saw Kari for the first time. She had waltzed out of the birth canal with the presence of a CEO entering a boardroom. With her enormous, bright eyes and mesmerizing smile, she demanded immediate attention. Within minutes of her birth, I was snapping Polaroids, determined to capture every moment of this new and miraculous experience, and to share it with all of my friends, colleagues, and relatives.

The next day, I grabbed anyone and everyone I could find and showed them these fantastic pictures of the newborn addition to our lives. After several hours of this, a close friend finally got the courage to come up to me and ask me to take a second look. "Lu, I think you need to study those pictures a little more closely."

I did. I saw what I'd seen all along—a beautiful 20-and-a-half-inch girl with dynamite eyes and a fabulous presence. I couldn't relate to his concern.

"Look one more time," he insisted.

Finally I understood what he and all the others had seen. The pictures I'd snapped had been taken immediately after birth. There were residual traces of blood all over Kari. It may have bothered everyone else, but it didn't matter to me. Within a few weeks, I sent one of her first at-home pictures off to a new service that produced 2-by-3-foot posters. It wasn't enough for me to have a 5-by-7-inch picture on my desk—I had to have the bigger-than-life-size version.

Kari, covered in blood. The image chilled me. Somewhere in the depths of this ugly hospital she was covered in blood again.

And still the slides continued to flash, one after the other.

Snapshots of a little girl beaming, dressed in her blue pajama suit, standing in our walk-in closet in Mexico...

Kari, her head thrown back, laughing devilishly in my lap...

All the animals on her bed and that wonderful smile she always greeted us with when we came in to wake her from her nap...

An older Kari shooting baskets or dribbling a soccer ball...

Kari, standing on the beach at Pajaro Dunes with that reflective, introspective look of hers...

Kari with Danny, the first time she included a boyfriend in a family event...

Kari, getting off the bus from Supercamp with Zach. It suddenly seemed like she wasn't such a kid anymore...

✳ ✳ ✳ ✳ ✳

"Lu, can you get up? I have to take Jessica down to the emergency room. She's freaking out. I don't want to leave you. I want to be here when the doctors come out with the report on Kari. But Jessica needs help. I'll be back as soon as I can."

I partially opened my eyes. Gin was kneeling beside me, trying to wake me, her face weary and drawn. My first thought was she had been a marvel throughout that terrible night. Even in the midst of her tears, there had been focus and composure. But now there was a new crisis.

"Lu, it's Jessica. She almost passed out a few minutes ago, and now she's feeling really sick. I think the shock of the accident has finally hit her."

"Where is she?" I asked.

"She's still in the bathroom. I'm going to try to talk to her, but I don't think we can handle all this alone. I need to take her down to the emergency room and get her admitted."

"Maybe her parents should come and get her…"

"I don't know…I think she really wants to be here for Kari…" Gin shook her head and took a deep breath. "Look, Lu, I think you need to call one of our friends. How about Ty and Nadine? Ask them if they can come give us a hand."

"Yeah, okay. Good idea."

I rose stiffly and as I headed for the payphone, I glanced at the clock: 3:00 A.M.

Since we didn't have any family in Los Angeles, we turned to Ty and Nadine Bobit, friends we knew through YPO, the Young Presidents Organization. The phone rang four times. Ty's groggy voice answered, "Hello?"

"Ty, it's Lu…"

"Lute? What time is it? Are you okay?"

"Listen, Kari's been in a serious accident. We're here at the hospital. Do you think that you and Nadine could…"

"Oh my God! Is Kari badly hurt?"

"No one really seems to know exactly what she's facing…but…yeah, it's bad."

"Oh man, I'm sorry. Where are you?"

"The trauma center at Harbor-UCLA."

"We'll be right there."

As promised, our friends were there in no time, stocked with pillows and blankets. Their very presence in the room lifted our spirits dramatically. By then Gin had succeeded in calming Jessica with the help of the emergency room, and she now got her settled down with Laurie. Along with Kristin and Kendra, the four of them stretched out to try to get to sleep. Ty and Nadine told us that, frighteningly, when they had gone by our house the front door was wide open and all the lights were on in the house.

Gin and I sat down with Ty and Nadine, trying to fill them in about all that had happened. As the others talked, my mind began to wander again. For the first time I began to ask myself about the sixteen-year-old kid who had hit Kari's car.

It's unbelievable; he should have avoided the accident. He's responsible for this mess. I need to contact a lawyer. I'll file suit the first thing tomorrow morning.

I didn't stay with that train of thought for very long. The truth of the matter was that Kari was more responsible for the accident than he was. She'd made the U-turn. She hadn't looked. No matter what he was doing, it was her fault. It was my fault. Had our relationship been better, Kari might have been in another place that night, that hour, that minute...

*   *   *   *   *

Uninvited, the slide show continued with another series of snapshots. Kari packing her bags. Kari saying goodbye at LAX. Kari, on the big 747, leaving for Sydney.

I had been very enthusiastic in encouraging Kari to have a study-abroad experience after her junior year in high school. I imagined an adventure in Spain, Mexico, or South America where she could hone her language skills. Kari looked into those programs with mild interest. But her eyes sparkled the brightest when she began to dream about Down Under—Australia.

With her usual determination, she discovered a program with experiences that attracted her and quickly decided Australia was the place for her. She made the journey and enjoyed an incredible amount of freedom for six weeks. At seventeen, she had already begun to feel she was ready to be totally independent from her parents. For six blissful weeks she lived out that kind of independence and it changed her dramatically.

The problem was, when she came back home, Kari returned to an unchanged household. Warren Bennis, the noted writer on leadership, has always said it is a crime to send a changed person back to an unchanged environment. If only I had understood that then.

Another snapshot…

When Kari was a little kid and had done something wrong, I'd draw an X on the floor where she had to sit cross-legged. I would then sit on the floor across from her so we could literally see eye-to-eye. The eye contact and close physical proximity allowed us to connect emotionally. We could talk unhindered about what had happened and come to an understanding.

Less than two weeks before the accident, we'd had a family conference in the big overstuffed chairs in our living room. That afternoon, I could sense Kari had wanted the old connection to be made with me. She needed the X on the floor. She needed to look Dad in the eye and get his full attention. But that time I couldn't get there emotionally; I was just too burdened, too wrapped up in my own problems to get focused on hers.

That night Kari had bolted out the door. She'd gone to stay with a friend. She hadn't come home.

✳ ✳ ✳ ✳ ✳

Ty had left to drive Kristin and Kendra home. I glanced at Nadine and Gin, deep in conversation. I squirmed around in the orange plastic chair, trying to get comfortable. The clock said 3:45. My mind returned to the sixteen-year-old boy who had hit Kari. Did he know how badly she was hurt? Did he blame himself? Should he?

We'd lived for two years in Mexico and became fascinated with the Spanish for "I broke it," *sè rompio*. In the Spanish language, the phrase means literally, "It is broken." The responsibility for the act is not given to anyone: Things are just broken. No matter how many times I flirted with blame that night I was able to stay away. Yes, I had responsibility. Yes, Kari had responsibility. Yes, the driver of the other car had responsibility. But the reality was that our daughter was seriously hurt. Blame was a nonissue.

Kari was broken. *Sè rompio.*

My thoughts again shifted. How much was all this going to cost? More to the point, how was I going to pay for it?

A bolt of electricity shot through my body. Acid welled up in my throat. I was suddenly aware that brain surgery alone costs hundreds of thousands of dollars and considering all the other complications, we were potentially facing a million-dollar bill. In that same instant I was stricken with the notion that, in leaving Evernet, I hadn't completed the right paperwork. What if I somehow hadn't extended my coverage? It would, quite simply, mean my financial ruin.

I forced my mind into "fix-it" mode, trying to diminish my anxiety, but it was not very comforting. I had enough personal resources to probably pay several hundred thousand dollars, but it would mean starting all over again after a fairly successful twenty-year career.

I could get some fund-raising events put together...

I could borrow against my home equity...

All mental roads led to the fact that if I hadn't done the paperwork, I was going to be starting over. This was not something I wanted to share with Gin that night. *I'm going to have to suck it up for now.*

Just then, a doctor came into the room. "Mr. and Mrs. Nussbaum, your daughter is still in surgery. But could you come with me for just a moment?"

He took us to a small room adjacent to the waiting room. "I want to talk to you about enrolling your daughter in two clinical trials. The first is a study of the key factors determining successful recovery from brain injuries…"

We signed up for that study without hesitation. The second was a bit more difficult. This was a double-blind study that would give half of the patients under study a real drug and half a placebo. The drug was an experimental steroid, nicknamed Lazaroid, which was designed to diminish post-surgical swelling. Swelling, as we later learned, is one of the most deadly side effects of brain trauma, and it can cause further stroke-like damage.

We signed the papers. Was it a wise decision? I wasn't thinking clearly and soon began to second-guess myself about that, too.

It was a long surgery and as Dr. Holland had predicted, a long, long night. Six hours of surgery, when you know the condition of the person and the likely outcome, can seem like an eternity. When you don't really know much about what's going on and you have no idea about the results, the wait is intolerable. We watched bad TV. We stared at the clock's second hand. We tried to sleep. Mostly we continued to lapse into personal reflection.

Yes, I told myself for the umpteenth time that night, in recent months I had become far too self-absorbed. I had taken time off the job search and gone skiing for weeks, then obsessed about my next career move, worried about the future of Luther Nussbaum. Suddenly I had two far more important concerns—the life of my daughter and the preservation of our family. Without question, I was going to have to put my problems and myself on hold for a few weeks. Maybe it was about time I did anyway.

It might sound strange, but we did not yet know what we had lost. If Kari had died instantly from the collision, we could have started grieving. If she'd had a broken arm, we could have prepared ourselves for six weeks of Kari in a cast and pin. But there in the waiting room the unknown and the unimaginable kept us in an utterly helpless state. We knew Kari's situation was serious—critical and perhaps even grave—but we had no concept about the scope of her injuries. In the meantime, there was nothing we could do but wait and hope for the best. It still hadn't hit me there was a good chance we would never talk to Kari again.

Above all else, I desperately wanted information that night. Questions repeated themselves in my mind again and again: *What is her real condition? How long will it take her to recover? Will she make it to graduation? Can we still get her into Boulder? How is the surgery going?*

The clock continued to move in slow motion. The girls stirred restlessly on the floor, never really quite asleep. I had seen brain surgery on the Discovery Channel. All at once I envisioned Kari on the operating table, with the surgeons around her. It nearly killed me.

At long last, the clock moved a bit past five, and the neurosurgeon, Duncan McBride, appeared at the door. "Mr. and Mrs. Nussbaum?"

As one, we jumped to our feet and rushed over to meet him. "Is she…? How is she?"

Looking drawn and drained, the doctor drew a deep breath and ran his fingers through his hair. "Well," he began, "things are better than we had initially thought. Kari did have a large hematoma, as we expected. But underneath it things weren't as bad as feared from the CAT scan."

"Thank God. What about everything else?"

"There were no signs of internal bleeding and her pelvis appears to be okay. However, her leg is badly broken. We've turned her over to a team of orthopedic surgeons to begin working on her femur. They're going to have to put a titanium rod in her leg. It's severely damaged, but I think we can save it. It will probably be another couple of hours of surgery."

"What's her prognosis?" I prodded.

The doctor paused, studying my face for a moment. "Mr. Nussbaum, your daughter has a serious brain injury. It's impossible to predict the ultimate outcome of injuries like hers. I'd like to tell you more about the future, to paint a positive picture for you, but all I can say is that we've completed the surgery successfully…"

"Thank you so much," Gin said.

Gin and I looked into each other's faces as if each was expecting the other to say something. Finally I spoke, "We need to call our families."

"I can't…" Gin said, clearly not able to make the calls in her emotional state.

Before making the calls, I went back to my orange chair and collapsed into it. The first thing that came to my mind was my sister, Lisha. Her son had been oxygen-deprived at birth. He had survived but with severe cerebral palsy. Many times I had watched my sister caring for her son Marc, and had told myself that I could never make it through something as difficult as that. Now, here I was, smack in the middle of a situation that could prove to be every bit as bad, if not worse.

I really didn't want to call my family and bring them news of another misfortune. Yet they needed to know. I honestly don't remember the content of any of the calls. As I talked with my family, I'm sure I shared with them my relief in hearing that Kari's situation was much better than the doctors had initially thought. But in truth, only one thing was going through my mind. I was trying to prepare myself for seeing Kari for the first time since the accident.

At about 8:30 A.M. a nurse came out into the waiting area. "Mr. and Mrs. Nussbaum, you can go and see your daughter now, but you'll have to go in one at a time."

Gracious as always, Gin let me go first. I followed the nurse through some hallways. She stopped in front of the Intensive Care Unit and pointed toward the door: "She's in there."

I stood in front of the door and collected myself. I tried to brace myself for the worst. I took a deep breath and turned the knob.

Nothing on earth could have prepared me for what met my eyes and ears. I had last seen Kari vibrant, sassy, and very alive, just the evening before. Now all I saw was white. All I heard was the beeping and pumping of machines. I don't know what I was expecting, but the reality of the situation crushed me. I wanted to sit down and bury my head in my hands, but there was no place to sit. I wanted to cry, but I was unable to release my tears.

A small, frail-looking body lay very still on a bed. There was a large bandage around her head. Her eyes were closed. Her face looked so unscarred, serene, and peaceful I was concerned she had crossed over into the next life. The only reason she was breathing was because of the ventilator rhythmically inhaling and exhaling for her.

Kari was barely alive.

CHAPTER THREE

Matters of Life and Death

I had been standing at Kari's bedside just a few seconds when one of the nurses walked over next to me for a moment. "How are you doing?" she asked quietly.

How am I doing? I looked at her blankly and mumbled some sort of response. After listening to the mechanical sound of Kari's breathing a little longer—knowing very well that she was only breathing with the help of the ventilator—I rejoined Gin outside. "Your turn, " I said to her.

"There are some new people looking for you in the waiting room," she replied. I squeezed her arm, shook my head, and walked back down the hall.

As I entered the waiting area, my eyes scanned the crowd of friends who had gathered there. By now the group numbered more than twenty. The news about Kari had quickly spread, almost as if there had been a news helicopter and a special camera crew on the spot. Friends had called friends who had called other friends. Each came to the hospital for a different reason. Some wanted news. Others came to support Kari or Gin or me.

They each wanted hope. I wanted understanding. My vacant stare imposed an effective wall to keep out their questions, but it denied me their physical and emotional comfort—support I really needed.

Once again, images of Kari involuntarily began to replay in my head. Kari, the most beautiful baby I'd ever seen. Kari, a precocious, ever-smiling toddler. Kari, the energetic, enthusiastic schoolgirl, racing at top speed into the house, slamming the door behind her. I forced the rerun to switch off and walked back out into the hall. I spoke to a nurse who was standing near there, checking a chart. "I wish there were a chair in my daughter's recovery room so my wife and I could sit in there with her."

"Actually," the nurse smiled, "we've found that patients like your daughter do better with less stimulation. I'm sorry it's not more comfortable for you."

She went on to explain that Kari's coma was like a deep sleep. Just as my own system was on sensory overload from the emotional trauma, the blunt trauma to Kari's nervous system had severely disrupted the physical processes in her brain. "The brain," she said, "tests itself one neural path at a time, and it is time-consuming and energy-draining. That's why the body shuts down its external interactions—to give itself time to test and repair."

Test and repair. I reflected on the idea—it was an interesting concept for me to contemplate right then. The doctors had filled me in on the nature of her injuries and how the surgery had gone. But what about the long-term prospects for Kari? What was next for her? I was already feeling a growing urge to help her get through this dark passage and into the light again. I had brought corporations back. I could bring my daughter back!

I tracked down Dr. Holland, a task that always seemed more difficult than we thought it should be. The world was *our* daughter's accident. How dare he be involved in other things of lesser importance?

"I want to know more about Kari's condition," I said to him, composing myself as carefully as possible.

He nodded. "Right now, she's holding her own. The brain is an intricate organ. Your daughter is indeed in a coma, but comas have gradations. Her pupils aren't responding to light and that's not a good sign. But when we removed the blood clot, we could see that there wasn't as much organ damage as we expected, based on the size of the hematoma."

My stomach tightened. *Her pupils don't respond to light. That can't be good.*

He went on. "You put Kari in the blind study for the new drug nicknamed Lazaroid, which is designed to keep the post-surgical swelling down. Right now, swelling can be one of the most deadly side effects of brain trauma. Our concentration is on preventing further damage."

He explained further that Kari was connected to an inter-cranial pressure (ICP) monitor. They left an open tube into Kari's cranial cavity. If the swelling exceeded a specified limit, the machine would summon a nurse to open the shunt and drain some of the fluid around the brain to quickly relieve the pressure before causing further damage.

"It's going to be a long haul," he said firmly, "not a sprint."

With that, Dr. Holland looked at his watch. Neither smiling nor frowning, his face wore the expression of practiced detachment. His manner was calculated, meant to remind me he wasn't a chaplain but a surgeon. He was trained to deal with the mechanics of the brain, not the emotional concerns of distressed family members.

"I'm sorry," he smiled faintly. "But I have to go now."

You may be saving Kari's life but you're killing my hope, I thought. *You may be talking long-term event, but I'm not up for spending several weeks in her recovery.* If only I had known that long-term was to be measured in years, not days and weeks.

I glumly walked back into the waiting room. The gathering parted to give me space. I slumped back into one of the awful plastic chairs, longing for Kari to wake up, just like in the movies. I imagined myself sitting next to her, feeling her squeeze my hand and hearing her familiar voice talking to me. I tried to shake off the fantasy. At the very least, I told myself, I needed information. I needed something to hang on to.

Just then Gin returned from surgical recovery room, her face almost as pale as Kari's. I ran to her and embraced her. It was a private moment in a very public venue. Both Kari's friends and ours were continuing to mass and now were spilling out into the hallway. Kids were sitting on their sweatshirts on the floor. Their faces were drawn, yet the day somehow seemed just a bit brighter; the air was crackling with the support of their energy.

But there were also tears and anxious faces searching ours for hope and answers. At that moment, we didn't have much to offer in terms of encouragement. All I could muster was, "The surgery went well. There's a lot less damage than expected." My spin was upbeat not because I was trying to give hope, but because I had heard hope in the doctor's report. No matter what the words, I always heard, or at least imagined, some glimmer.

It's amazing how little was said and how much was communicated. Several friends stood up and opened their arms in speechless expressions of love. Teenage girls squeezed together next to each other on the floor. Eventually, I turned to Gin and said, "I'm on serious overload. I need to go home and get a shower. Can you take over for a while?"

* * * * *

After my ill-fated run, a long shower was more than welcome. Warm water opened my pores and provided the first few moments of restoration. But as I dressed, the relief did not last long. Anxiety broke through again with all kinds of concerns that hadn't occurred to me before. How could I have missed them?

I was still sure that Kari would wake up soon, perhaps in the next day or two. But then what? What would happen next? Which doctor in our area was the best in the brain-trauma field? What kind of cutting-edge clinical research was emerging that we could tap into? I knew myself well enough to realize that the only way I could remove the deadly weight of uncertainty from my chest was by doing something. And the only thing I could do was study, learn, and make well-informed decisions.

I recalled that Harbor-UCLA had a medical library on site. As part of the UCLA system, it was an academic medical center. I finished dressing quickly, got in the car, and headed back to the hospital. That same afternoon, I located the library, and once inside I immediately started accumulating all the information I could find. A strategy for educating myself evolved quickly. I searched the library database for recent articles having anything to do with "subdural hematoma," "coma," and "traumatic brain injury." Unfortunately, the articles were written for clinicians and were barely intelligible to a layperson like myself. What was very clear, however, was the Hollywood portrayal of a sudden coma recovery was nothing more than movieland magic. It wasn't going to happen.

The medical community described the situation all too realistically. Both the Rancho Los Amigos and Glasgow Scales for measuring the state of the coma said it could take months for a person to go through the stages of "awakening." With every passing day, the probability of a successful outcome decreased dramatically. After one month, most people in a coma did not come back. After three months, almost no one did.

A chilling thought gripped me with icy fingers: *If Kari doesn't wake up pretty soon, she isn't likely to wake up at all.* I silenced the thought. I simply wasn't ready to face that possibility. It wasn't an option. I refused to envision Kari in a pro-longed comatose state, with nothing but a ventilator keeping her alive.

Outside of that academic environment, the only positives I could find were a few popular press stories, especially a *Reader's Digest* article about a man who had slowly but steadily recovered from a coma. I studied the story hungrily. It had taken him ten years to recover his memory. He had first thought that he was living in the house he'd lived in as child, but his awareness had gradually improved, in stages. I clutched the slender hope the article offered. Eventually, my wife wanted me to share the results of our research.

"Gin, I've copied some articles for you to read."

"Okay," she said, her voice a monotone.

"I've got some information here that we're going to need."

She nodded, but she wasn't really interested. "Can't you just tell me what it says?" she said. "I'm too tired to concentrate…"

I looked at her face and saw the pain in her eyes, the strain in her expression. I took a deep breath and summarized what I had read. I fudged the data and intertwined the popular press articles with the disciplined medical journal articles. I made it sound better than it was. Much better.

Of course I knew Gin could handle the bad news. Gin can handle anything. Even with her gracious and compassionate exterior, she is strong and sturdy at the core. The reason I didn't tell her everything was because I refused to believe what it said. I wasn't willing to accept the outcome that most of the current research predicted. Despite all of the negative information, I simply could not resign myself to all the negatives. I decided right then and there we would simply "will" Kari well with our hearts.

* * * * *

Throughout the afternoon and into the early evening, even more friends gathered. By midafternoon, there was a group of more than forty who had come to the hospital to be close to Kari. They were talking quietly, doing their best to support one another and encourage us. It was now Sunday. Monday would be Kari's eighteenth birthday. The kids went to work making a huge birthday banner for her. Kristin was convinced Kari, with her usual theatrical personality, would wake up on her birthday, April 5, and see the banner. They were all quite convinced she would be awake at any moment. It was a scenario I had already discarded, but I let them dream.

Meanwhile, Gin was concerned that the kids should have a way to express their feelings. She asked a friend to buy a book so they could write remembrances for Kari to read when she woke up. Kari had been an encourager to so many of her friends, always there for anyone who had an issue or a problem. Now her friends wanted more than anything in the world to encourage her. They filled a couple of notebooks with letters and notes. They also made tapes of music for her to listen to. Just about all of them really wanted to see her but the medical staff reminded me of the "no stimulation" rule. It hurt, but I had to tell those kids they couldn't go in. No exceptions.

* * * * *

Monday, her birthday, came and went. Kari was still asleep.

Late Sunday evening, Kari had been moved to the first of two intensive care units that were to be her home for the next month. The neurosurgical ICU had no space and so she was temporarily placed in an extremely overcrowded general ICU. At long last, on Tuesday morning, Kari was finally moved up to the eighth floor specialty ICU. Changing units meant that a whole new set of people would be working with Kari. We figured we would have to start from scratch to encourage the level of special care we wanted her to have. In the new ICU, they were prepared to handle brain-injured patients, but as we were to find out shortly, in a brain injury ward, death was ever present.

As I stood by Kari's side on Tuesday, a nurse came in. "Mr. Nussbaum, " she said, "we need to chat a minute."

Of course, my first response was alarm. But I quieted myself. "Sure," I said evenly. "What's going on?"

"I wanted to let you know there's a new patient coming into ICU. In fact, he's on his way from the ER right now."

"Why did you want me to know about him?"

"He's…he's also a teenager. He's just fifteen years old and he was hit by a car riding his bike to school for the first time. His parents had a helmet for him, but in his rush to get to school, he didn't put it on. A car ran a stop sign and hit him."

"My God!" I felt myself slumping. "Another kid on life support?"

"Look," she said. "That's why I wanted to talk to you. Yes, Kari's in a coma. But this boy is in far worse condition. There's a big difference. He has brain stem damage. Don't draw parallels. Don't let it get you down."

A blank stare belied my surge of emotion. I muttered, "I'll try."

Just then I heard elevator doors open and the sounds of activity moving down the hall as several orderlies rolled the boy in. I looked at him carefully. He was white just like Kari and connected to countless machines. But unlike Kari, he had no energy coming from his body. Somehow, I could feel the difference. I clung to it.

Moments later, his parents came down the hall and I watched as the same surgeon gave them the same clinical cold shoulder. I contemplated introducing myself, but could see they needed to be alone with their son. I stepped out and let them have the room to themselves.

A few minutes later, one of their friends came out of the elevator looking for them. He recognized me. We both lived in the same neighborhood.

We introduced ourselves. We had lived in the same area of Palos Verdes for years, but knew each other only by sight as a familiar face. Somehow transported to the waiting hallway of a neurosurgical ICU, we were suddenly long lost friends.

"Did you know my daughter is here?"

"Yes, I heard about it in the neighborhood," he said softly. "But I'm actually here to see my close friends. Their son was in a horrible accident."

"Yes, they just brought him in. He's in the ICU with Kari."

"I'm so sorry about your daughter," he said.

"Thank you. It's a parent's worst nightmare. I'm sorry about your friends' son, too."

"Many people are praying. I telephoned the family in Pakistan and they are going to sacrifice a lamb and have the meat distributed to the poor. It's a form of prayer to keep the cycle of life going. You should do it too."

"I wish them the best." What else could I say? I shook his hand and went back to sit with Gin.

On Thursday, I was in standing at Kari's bedside when I overheard one of the nurses on the phone. She was calling other hospitals to arrange for the donation of the boy's organs. She was working on the placement of his heart and was estimating when they expected to take him off life support. "Sometime tomorrow," I heard her say.

I froze.

Until that moment, death had never been a possibility for Kari. But in an instant, I realized she might die. I closed my eyes and shuddered. What if it were Kari's organs being donated? What if all hope was gone? Something like a bolt of electricity shot down my spine. I opened my eyes. Kari was still alive. The respirator was as rhythmic as before.

Unknown to us, our friends had increased their time at the hospital since this other teenage accident victim had arrived. They were very concerned about the potential impact his death might have on us.

The next day, the boy's parents came in with several of their friends and stood beside his bed. By the time the life-support equipment had been disconnected, everyone was in tears. It was a heartbreaking scene, one I will never forget. Yet, in a strange way, their situation seemed more merciful than ours. They had a resolution. We had purgatory.

Although I do not practice any form of religion, I was brought up in a very religious family, and I remain deeply spiritual. I am convinced I have been given the power to change the things I can change and the courage to accept the things I cannot change. In that terrible hour, as the boy's family grieved, I knew we would fight for Kari with all the resources we could summon within ourselves.

And—in spite of the odds, in spite of the medical pessimism—I knew we would prevail. Or was it just hope?

* * * * *

From the earliest hours of her hospitalization, I had assumed Kari could hear me in some way. My deepest longing was to help her reconnect to the world. At times, I thought I felt her struggling to make the choice between giving in or going on. Maybe it was a few little flinches around the corners of her eyes that I noticed. Or maybe it was just my own passionate desire for her recovery.

I imagined her as a climber on Mount Everest in a blinding snowstorm. Would she have the courage to continue to put one foot in front of the other, to walk frostbitten the last 3,000 yards, step by agonizing step, back to her base camp?

And what about the journey for Gin and me? What would we consider to be a "positive outcome"? At that point, just to see our daughter alert enough to give a yes/no communication by the wink of an eye or the squeeze of a hand would have been a huge gift. Even to get that, we would have to invest a lot and anticipate little in return. To lower our expectations that far was a tremendous struggle for both of us. We wanted so much.

People were praying for Kari, with several local church congregations as well as people of various faiths volunteering to send spiritual energy her way. But I could not pray. My world of belief was more complicated. Were things caused by God or by some other force beyond the power of man to explain? I could not say. I wanted, but did not demand. I hoped, but did not expect. Still the feeling persisted that if enough people made an emotional investment in Kari, eventually it would come back to us.

Having missed her birthday, Kristin now became convinced Kari would wake up on Easter Sunday. She had such a belief in this idea, she dragged me along with her. When Easter came and nothing happened, I went numb. Kari had not awakened. I couldn't make it better. I couldn't reverse the coma's course. I couldn't cry. I was highly emotional, but tears offered me no release. I stared. I walked. I churned intellectually and wrestled emotionally. My mind works in decision trees. I went down every decision branch looking for options where I could *do something*. Ultimately, I came to see the only thing I could control was my attitude.

Meanwhile, Gin was doing her best. At first she wept a lot, but she soon pulled herself together to direct her energy toward caring for Kari. She brought in Kari's senior picture, taken before the accident, which so wonderfully captured Kari's spirit. There she was, tossing her head, flinging her hair back flirtatiously. Gin passed this picture around the nursing staff and taped it to Kari's headboard. She wisely believed that by giving the clinical staff a glimpse of Kari's vibrancy and beauty they would be more motivated to help in her recuperation. I can only imagine what it is like to see severely damaged human beings in a dozen beds day after day. We wanted Kari's caretakers to see her as a real person with high spirits, a captivating smile, and a strong personality.

* * * * *

During those early days, our friends took care of all of our meals. Anyone who expressed an interest in doing something for us was enlisted to rustle up a dinner. It was at least six weeks after the accident before we had to worry about cooking. And in the ICU waiting room, we were rarely alone. As we sat outside for hours to get in a few minutes with Kari, our friends' company helped us keep our spirits intact, so we could pass our strength on to Kari.

I wished we could have let more of our friends in to see Kari. They certainly deserved it for all the support they were providing us. But the ICU was a medium-sized open ward with about a dozen other patients, no room for visitors, and a high risk of infection. Still, after about a week, we lobbied for Kari's two best friends, twins, to go in to see her. Jill stood on the right side with Mimi on the left. I was watching Mimi, when all of sudden Jill felt faint. Without thinking, trying to keep herself from falling, she grabbed Kari's leg. In the process, she nearly pulled her out of bed and onto the floor. I was horrified. I realized right then and there that no one else would be able to see her until she was much, much better.

The hospital itself had its own ways of discouraging visitors. Harbor-UCLA was a Los Angeles County hospital. Often the patients in the neurological ICU were gang members who had suffered gunshot wounds to the head. For obvious reasons, the hospital staff wanted to minimize the number of gang members hanging around, so they put only four chairs down the hallway from the ICU, outside the medical conference room. Thus, we waited on cold, plastic seats across from the ever-opening elevator door. No private tears for Ginger. No comfort for either of us.

*   *   *   *   *

One afternoon, a few days after the accident, I was in the ICU talking with one of the residents. My back was to Kari, and I was standing several feet away from her bed.

Suddenly, the resident exclaimed, "Oh my God!"

I turned around in time to see Kari sit up, then lie back down again.

The resident went over, lifted her arms, and tested some pressure points on her elbows. No response. He reached up and gently placed his fingers on the jugular vein on her throat.

"It's okay," he said. "She's still asleep."

"What was that?" I asked, feeling shocked and shaken.

"Involuntary muscle reflex. That's why I checked several reflex spots. To see if it was continuous."

"And?"

"It's not."

"It sure gave me an adrenaline surge."

"I know," he chuckled. "Me, too. There might be some more of them."

"What do you mean?"

"It's called 'agitation.' It's a sign the body is working on things."

"Working on things? Does this mean she's about to…" My voice couldn't disguise the sudden burst of hope I was feeling.

"Don't go there," he said. "I'm telling you."

His pager went off and he had to go.

As we continued to read and learn from experiences, we were to watch Kari struggle through days, even weeks of agitation: "marching" in bed and hours of record-breaking tummy crunches. While agitation was a great sign of progress, it was extraordinarily painful to watch. The great progress along Kari's road back was agonizing to our family.

Ginger was so wonderfully successful at integrating fully and transparently with the staff in the ICU. She worked like a secret agent, infiltrating the hospital system in her extraordinarily friendly way, making use—to our advantage—of the pecking order that exists among interns, residents, and doctors.

We had learned quickly how things work at a teaching hospital. To become a full-fledged neurologist involves a very specific sequence of ascent. In the first two years, interns are rotated through multiple preparatory disciplines. We discovered that since the two-year residents were not specialists, they were not yet conditioned to be aloof with patients. They would talk with us at some length about comas and brain conditions. We would then use this information to lobby the more knowledgeable five-year residents, then work our way up to negotiating information from the supervising neurologist.

We did all we could to get Kari the best care possible, within the rules, procedures, and limitations of an ICU. We were not permitted to spend too much time with her, however, because she was in an open ICU ward with a dozen other severely brain-injured patients. Also, she was still being monitored by the Hewlett-Packard ICP monitor, measuring the pressure caused by the swelling of the brain. Stimulation of any sort could cause her ICP to rise.

Every time we went in to see her, we had to keep one eye on Kari and one eye on her ICP number. As we touched her, held her, drew her to us, and worked on her range of motion, the ICP would soar. The nurse would open her shunt valve and drain fluid from her brain. We struggled between our fear of causing further damage and our fear of allowing her to drift further away.

And despite her controlled surroundings, we were still rarely allowed to stay with her for more than a few minutes at a time. We used those minutes to tell her stories, and we left behind tapes of music she had once enjoyed. We skirted the conflict—we tugged on her with reasons to come back to the living, while keeping everything absolutely quiet so her brain could regenerate its ability to function, one connection at a time.

We often felt intense frustration, wanting desperately to hold Kari in our arms, to draw her back to us by the sheer force of human contact. But every time we touched her or talked to her, the ICP number would begin to rise and with it the realization that our "loving" her might actually do more harm than good.

* * * * *

An ICU is a notorious breeding ground for disease. During the first few days of hospitalization, Kari had battled several infections. But during the second week her fever started to go down. Even more encouraging to me, her right eye began to open occasionally. I wondered if somehow, someway she could see me. At first, although the eye opened, it didn't seem to be looking at anything. But several days later, Kari's eye remained open more of the time, and sometimes I was convinced it had blinked in response to my questions. This was my first struggle with isolating perceptive insight from wishful thinking.

We also noticed Kari seemed to be more active in the mornings than the evenings. Gin and I reminded each other that she always had been a morning person. And when one of us touched on her foot or arm, she reacted, by jerking her leg. *Is this a real reaction or an involuntary reflex of a muscle? Are we feeling her returning presence or it is this just another case of projecting parents?* These were questions we asked ourselves over and over in the coming months.

I leaned over and quietly said to Gin, "You know, seeing Kari move like that…"

"I think it's paying off, Luther. All the time and energy we're spending with her."

"Maybe we'll get our daughter back after all," I said.

The nurse must have heard us because she walked over and gave me the familiar refrain, "Take it slow."

That afternoon, I saw what she meant. At 8:30 in the morning, Kari had looked strong. By 1:30 that afternoon she seemed tired and wan. I asked the nurse about it.

"Well," she said, "she's still running a low-grade fever, about 100 degrees. You'd get worn-out, too, if you'd had a fever for nearly two weeks."

"Yeah."

"I need you to step out of the room while I clean her breathing tubes. It's not a pretty procedure."

"Can't I watch from across the room?" I pleaded. "I'll put on a mask."

"Well….Here you go."

She tossed me a mask from the box on the counter.

Watching the cleaning of the tubes was gruesome to us. The nurse disconnected the ventilator and then worked a smaller tube down inside of Kari's ventilator tube toward her lungs. Kari spasmed involuntarily in reaction. I wrenched in empathetic support. She was in such a deep coma she could not react to a marching band or a helicopter flying close by but the process was so invasive she could not help but show major reaction. Once the inner tube was in place the suctioning began along with new spasms. No wonder they preferred we were not there when they suctioned her lungs!

Once the procedure was over, after she buttoned Kari up, she took off her mask and opened the door. A physical therapist came in and said she was going to start Kari on an exercise program. Even though Kari could not move by herself, the activity would prevent muscular atrophy. The therapist, Janie, put Kari's legs and arms through range-of-motion exercises to help maintain tone. Given Janie's schedule, she could not consistently range Kari as many times a day as she needed to be ranged. She taught us how to keep the defensive tone from attacking Kari's range of motion. This was to be another constant battle during the coming months.

By about 2:30 each day, we all saw Kari lose energy. She became increasingly pale and washed-out. So we all packed up and left her alone for the rest of the day.

Still, deep inside, I knew well we were seeing positive change. There was progress. There was improvement. There was hope. There really was hope.

Little by little, I cautioned myself, trying my best to stifle a smile, trying not to get too excited. From our new baseline of a comatose Kari, each improvement was a miracle. *Stay away from visions of who Kari was before the accident. She is dead. Stay focused on the new Kari in front of you. She's alive. Take it easy, Luther. Little by little.*

CHAPTER FOUR

New Beginnings

In the days that followed, in spite of Kari's lengthening stay in ICU, hope arrived in small bundles. While we were fighting the reality of the medical reports, Kari kept giving us small but important signs of improvement. We were spending increasing amounts of time in the ICU with Kari, and her ICP finally was not rising constantly above the threshold. This emboldened us to talk with her more and more.

One morning, after sitting with Kari for a while, I stood up again and studied her face. I again thought for sure she was trying to signal me with her eyes. Not in any sense that most people would understand; her stare was the vacant stare of one who is blind. Her eyes were open but there was no movement of recognition. Yet beyond her vacant stare was something, something I saw or felt. Or did I? I was never able to get a consistent response to my signals, which left me in a now-familiar state of uncertainty. Was Kari really beginning to respond? Or was my imagination again playing tricks on me?

By late afternoon, Kari's friends began to gather, as some had done every day since she was first hospitalized. School was out for the day. They sat on the cold floor for hours, looking up when the double doors opened, leading down the long hall to the brain injury ICU. They were hoping for good news, anticipating the wonderful moment when someone would show up and say, "Kari's awake now, and she wants you to come in and see her."

We're all victims of hope, I thought as I watched their expectant faces. *Or maybe we're all beneficiaries of hope. Kari has come so far.*

Daily, the friends spent hours composing letters to her in notebooks and on writing tablets. At first, so many people came to visit Kari the nurses opened up a conference room just to house them all. However, after the initial uncertainties surrounding Kari's survival were resolved, and once everyone learned Kari could not have any visitors, fewer of her friends stopped by. They still came, but in smaller numbers. There were consistently three, four, or five supportive friends around at most times of the day, with many more than that arriving at peak visiting hours.

One night, two of Kari's stalwart supporters got a surprising reward for their troubles. A resident opened Kari's door to roll her downstairs for one of her periodic CAT scans and seeing the kids there, asked if they would like to talk to Kari while she waited for the elevator. I don't know what they said to her or whether they saw something flicker in her eyes the way I did, but the resident told me later the kids were delighted by the opportunity. How touched we were to learn that afterward, several kids waited all day for another chance to say something personal and special to Kari.

＊ ＊ ＊ ＊ ＊

Kari's mostly clean CAT scan was the most helpful and encouraging bit of concrete information Gin and I had received since the accident. Then, not long afterward, the head nurse surprised me again. In fact, she asked me something that quite thoroughly astonished me. I was standing in the ICU near the nurses' central station while one of the many procedures was being done to her, when the nurse casually inquired, "So where are you going to move Kari for her rehab?"

"Rehab?" I stammered. "What do you mean?"

"Well, I'm sure you know that rehab is the next step," she smiled.

I was taken aback, and I'm sure my tone reflected it. "Look, as you know, Kari's on a ventilator, being monitored minute by minute for her ICP. We can't even go near her for fear we'll increase her brain damage. How in the hell could she possibly be moved to a rehab center?"

"It's just something you're going to need to think about," she shrugged, looking—I thought—a little smug.

"My God," I shook my head. "Kari isn't even awake. Can't you just keep giving her physical therapy right here? What's the point of moving her at this stage?"

"Well..."

"We had no idea she would have to move to a different hospital, " I rambled.

"Well," the nurse continued, "if I were you, I would definitely go visit several rehab facilities and get an idea of what they offer. That way you can make an informed decision when the time comes. It's just a suggestion, of course. Maybe it's something you and you wife can do in your spare time."

* * * * *

Gin was more matter-of-fact about finding a rehab facility for Kari than I was. Without much ado, she simply volunteered to make the initial scouting trips. And off she went, taking along a good friend, Suzi Mikos. After two days of exploration, however, Gin returned with a less-than-enthusiastic report.

"Lu," she said, her face etched with sadness, "all we saw were either homes for the elderly or—worse than that—warehouses for the terminally unconscious. It's so depressing!"

"Why was it so depressing?" I pressed her for more details, wanting the news to be better, more hopeful.

"There was one…" she paused, searching for words. Gin was in shell shock. "Luther, you wouldn't have believed it. They had three patients to a room, all lined up and all on respirators."

"Sounds like a parking lot."

"More like a living morgue," she groaned. "How can they do that to people?"

"I suppose they have nowhere else to put them. Still, it sounds really gross."

"Oh, God. I can't even describe it. If depression has a smell, I got a serious dose of it today."

"I don't see Kari in a place like that," I said, as firmly as possible.

"No way! I'll take care of her myself at home before I'll put her in a place like that." We had seen the placement of a hospital bed in the middle of the living room in the movie *Lorenzo's Oil.*

"It sounds to me like some of these places have no interest in their patients' improvement. They're just collecting rent."

Gin put her hand on my arm. "All I know is, we've got to find something better for Kari. That's all there is to it."

"I'm sure there are more options. Did you go to every place on the list we put together?"

"No, I didn't. Fortunately, there are several more left," she sighed. "Surely some of them are better."

The next morning, Gin and I went together to see Rancho de Los Amigos, in Downey. Our first reaction was relief. We were thoroughly impressed with the professional caretakers' expertise in rehabilitating brain-injured patients. Their approach was active, entailing large doses of physical therapy, much like the care Kari was presently receiving at Harbor-UCLA. The reputation of Rancho de Los Amigos is well known around the world.

That same afternoon, we went to Casa Colina, which is located in Palos Verdes, not very far from our home. It, too, offered a well-conceived rehabilitation program. Casa Colina's team believed in a lot of quiet time, limiting the amount of activity for brain-injured patients.

Both Rancho de Los Amigos and Casa Colina were achieving positive results, which caused us some confusion. We really didn't know as much as we should have about what brain injury rehab entails. We decided to keep gathering information and to make the decision only when we had to. Till then, Kari was in good hands at Harbor-UCLA.

✱ ✱ ✱ ✱ ✱

One afternoon, in an effort to explore every possible option, Gin telephoned the Brain Injury Foundation to ask for help in finding the right facility for Kari. For some unexplainable reason, they didn't keep a list of facilities. Worse yet, they sounded like they didn't even want to take her call. How could they remain so aloof, so disinterested in practical considerations? Their detachment was infuriating.

She also phoned the Southern California Brain Injury Association and didn't receive much help from them either. A machine answered and took her message on voicemail. After three days, there was still no returned phone call.

Even the Harbor-UCLA library did not have much on facilities for brain injury rehab. Well aware that we needed all the information we could possibly accumulate, we finally did it the old-fashioned way: networking. Fortunately, because of our association with Young Presidents Organization, we have an exceptionally large group of friends and associates. And we asked everyone we knew to call any and every physician they knew. The question: What should our priorities be regarding Kari's rehabilitation program?

Two days later, we got a phone call. "Check on Daniel Freeman Memorial Hospital's Rehabilitation Center," one of our friends suggested. "My doctor went there himself after a pretty serious operation. He swears by it." We received a second endorsement of Daniel Freeman from Lou Kwiker, who had used the facility for his own personal rehab.

"Daniel Freeman? Where's that?"

"Don't ask," he replied with a chuckle. "Let's just say it's not in the high-rent district."

The next day Gin drove over to take a look at the Daniel Freeman facility. She came back feeling ecstatic. "I can't believe how much better it is than most of the others. For one thing, it's pretty. It has some really attractive outdoor areas where the patients can go for wheelchair rides in the fresh air."

"Sounds like a country club."

She laughed. "Not exactly that nice, but I really like the surroundings. And I liked the therapists, too. They all seemed friendly and caring."

"What did they say about taking a patient in Kari's condition?" Our biggest problem was that Kari was still subacute. Most rehab facilities required their patients to have reached acute status.

"They offer both residential and outpatient services. Plus, they were willing to accept Kari as a subacute patient."

"It sounds pretty good," I said. "So I guess that means we have three places to choose from: Rancho de Los Amigos, Casa Colina, and Daniel Freeman."

"That's right. And I think I like Daniel Freeman the best. Long Beach Memorial would be on the list and a little closer if Kari were a bit further along."

During this period of time, we learned that paralleling the three facilities we were considering, there were three basic approaches to rehab:

1. Minimal stimulation. The intent was to keep the patient extremely quiet except during therapeutic sessions so that the brain would have time to heal. This translated into our spending very little time with Kari.

2. Sensory overload. This meant eight to ten patients on a ward with lots of stimulation, no privacy, and very little quiet time.

3. A combination approach.

Daniel Freeman offered the third option. But despite our preference for what sounded to us like a balanced program, we really weren't sure. After reading and rereading several brochures for the umpteenth time, I said, "Gin, I still don't know what's best for Kari."

"I know. How are we supposed to figure all this out for ourselves? As far as I can see, the doctors don't even agree. There are valid arguments for all three approaches."

"I guess it's simply up to us to make a decision...."

"...and take the consequences," Gin finished my thought.

"Okay," I said, "let's review the pros and cons of each place."

"Well, first of all, Rancho is one of the most respected facilities for brain injury recovery," Gin noted. "And according to those articles we read, they're staffed with some of the leading minds."

"That's true. And it counts for a lot," I said. "But they said they wouldn't put Kari into rehab. They'd start her first in the hospital ward."

"And that doesn't make sense when she'll have to travel so far over to the rehab facility for her exercise. I can't see her doing that once or twice a day."

"No, it doesn't. She's not ready to be moved."

"I agree," Gin nodded.

"And Rancho is far away from our house. It would be a long drive every day. It would burn up a lot of our energy."

"And," Gin commented, "they use a group-housing model, multiple patients to a room. Daniel Freeman has private rooms as well as daily access to physicians. *And* they are also ranked 'exceptional' as a brain injury ward," Gin noted.

"You've been reading my research reports!" I laughed, impressed by her burst of technical expertise.

"I've been doing some digging of my own," she smiled.

"So what's the problem with Freeman?"

"Well," Gin said, "there's its location. It's three blocks from the Forum…"

"…in the heart of South Central."

"Yeah, and it hasn't been that long since the riots. Less than a year. What if the neighborhoods explode again and we can't get in to see her? Will her friend's parents allow them to visit her? Some of them have already expressed concerns about the drive to Harbor-UCLA. What will they think of Daniel Freeman?"

"I don't think that's such a concern. Without riots, the neighborhoods near Freeman seem peaceful and safe. I don't think that will be an issue. The hospital should be safe under any condition. If anything happens we'll get in and just stay!"

"Well then," Gin summed up, "it looks like it comes down to a choice of treatment plans. Daniel Freeman has individual rooms combined with a group activity ward. That would give Kari the best of both approaches. There's that—plus the good feeling I got from the therapists."

"So what do you think?" Gin asked.

"Daniel Freeman it is!"

✱ ✱ ✱ ✱ ✱

Once we'd made that very difficult decision, we relaxed a little. However, the trauma of moving Kari was much greater than we anticipated. At Harbor we had cracked the code on how to get information—how to get specialized, extra efforts made on Kari's behalf. We had formed a working routine, and no matter how bad some days were, that routine had been comforting. The physical therapist had given her personal time to train us and to work with Kari. The staff was invested in her well-being. We couldn't help but wonder what lay ahead at Daniel Freeman. Who would connect with Kari like these people had? Could she really survive without intensive care?

While we were making the necessary arrangements for the move, Harbor prepared Kari's records for the new team that would be caring for her at Freeman. Meanwhile, word got around that Kari was moving. One by one, nurses and orderlies stopped by to wish us well. I hated to say goodbye to them, especially the young resident who had done such a sensational job of managing her slew of infectious diseases. He had played a key role in Kari's improvement. But more meaningful to us personally, he had checked on Kari every day. When he found out she was leaving, he showed up one afternoon. I could tell he was sad.

"I don't have any money for a big gift," he said, "but I want to give Kari something. How 'bout if I give her my hair band, to remember me by? It's used, but it's all I've got right now."

"Go ahead and put it in her hair," I said stepping back, feeling both touched and grateful.

This guy really cared. So did a lot of other people at Harbor. We would be losing all of that kindness, concern, and compassion once Kari got on the ambulance for the ride across town. Neither Gin nor I was looking forward to that loss.

* * * * *

Moving day arrived far too quickly. Only twenty-four hours after making the decision, a room at Daniel Freeman opened up. One minute we were folding blankets and peeling off the photographs we had taped to Kari's bedside. The next minute we were getting out of the way so the ambulance crew could get her on a Gurney and wheel her away.

Gin was nervous about the process of transporting Kari across town. It was certainly true she was frail and fragile, and we'd been handling her with great gentleness, only to uproot her abruptly and subject her to a certain amount of jarring and jolting. But I was more sanguine than Gin about the move. It was traumatic for all of us, to be sure, but I never feared for Kari's survival. It was a short trip—no more than 7 or 8 miles—and the ambulance had all the plugs and jacks for her life-support machines. I faced the moving process with logic and simply willed myself not to be afraid.

Gin rode in the front seat with Kari in the ambulance. I followed in the car. Our little caravan drove off into a whole new unknown world.

* * * * *

Before we knew it, Kari was being rolled upstairs to room 218 at Daniel Freeman's Rehabilitation Center. Although I was concerned about a dozen other things, Gin noticed the room was decorated in shades of pink and gray, and mentioned she thought it looked pretty.

Good room for a girl, I told myself in passing. *Quite a contrast to our early attempts to be gender neutral by giving Kari barns, things colored blue, and cars as opposed to the stereotypical dolls, dollhouses, and pinks.*

The new staff came in, one by one, introduced themselves, and gave Kari the once-over. And they surprised us with some new impressions of Kari. They felt positive about the shape she was in, which probably says more about what kind of broken bodies they'd seen before than about how well she was doing. Still, we were glad to hear the optimism in their voices. For us, it was a bright, sunny occasion to see Kari out of the hospital and into rehab.

* * * * *

We had another daughter at home. Kristin had been forced to grow up prematurely. A month shy of her sixteenth birthday her sister was taken from her. Kristin wasn't prepared for an adult experience with death. Her big sister was a risk-taker, an extrovert, and an adventurer. Kari was admired. No, their relationship was not always smooth. Kari was occasionally cruel to her younger sister. Kristin had even taken a joy in seeing the police car coming up the night of the accident. Moments later, Kristin had to adjust her life dramatically. Her first way of coping with the tragedy was to deny it, to try to go on with her life as though nothing had happened.

Kari's accident was in early April. It wasn't until the end of April that we got around to replacing the totaled Previa van. We elected to buy a Jeep. We figured we would find a vehicle that could do fair battle with an Explorer. As Kristin's sixteenth birthday on May 6 approached, Kristin announced to us one day, "Don't even think about not letting me get my driver's license. You're not going to protect me from a fate like Kari's." We admired her spunk but we really wanted to encapsulate our only remaining daughter with a voice. On her birthday, Gin's mom took Kristin down to the California Department of Motor Vehicles for a very early morning driver's test. She passed. She was liberated. Gin and I were petrified. Lightning doesn't strike twice in the same place, does it?

Within days, Kristin was on the phone. "Mom and Dad, you don't mind if I drive Christy over to her dad's house? He lives close to Disneyland." *Mind? Three freeways and 30 miles? Our living daughter at risk. God, please give us strength to go on living.*

"Kristin, how about if we take this a little bit at a time. Let's set up some zones. The first zone will be on the hill. Once that's mastered, then we can think about adding in the area around the base of the hill which will be zone two. Later we'll be ready for broader areas of L.A. Either your mom or I will drive you to Christy's dad's and then pick you up."

"Okay." One save, but our new life was not going to be easy. It was ironic we felt most safe with her driving in the exact location where Kari'd had her accident.

* * * * *

Kari was soon settled in her new "world." In the minutes that followed, I walked down the halls at Daniel Freeman, hearing my footsteps echoing slightly along the polished corridor. My mind carried me back to the drive across town, and as I remembered passing the Forum, I suddenly recalled taking Kari there on her twelfth birthday. It had been affectionately known as the "Fabulous Forum" in those days, and Kari had told me very specifically she wanted to go to a Laker's game to celebrate the occasion.

Anxious to make her birthday special, I had telephoned for tickets, somehow managing to get great seats, and with a sense of anticipation, had taken her to the game. I'd fully expected she and I would have a great time together. But instead of being her usual, ebullient self, for some reason Kari seemed edgy. I noticed her eyes scanning the arena from time to time, searching for something, looking at the scoreboard. I was puzzled and a little disappointed. I was also slightly annoyed.

Once we were buckled in the car and heading home, I asked, "So what was wrong with you tonight? You didn't seem like you were having a very good time. Why did you keep looking around the building? What were you looking for?"

Without the least hesitation, Kari said, "I was upset because I thought you would have us picked up in a limo. And I thought that 'Happy Birthday, Kari' would be flashed on the scoreboard."

I sighed and fell silent. That was my Kari, forever feisty, forever imaging very special occasions.

Now, out of nowhere as I paced that quiet hallway, powerful feelings swelled within me like a storm about to pound against a shore. I felt a rising need to get out—out of the hallway, out of the building.

I rushed to the elevator, pushed the ground floor button, and found my way out the front door. I had no idea where I was going or why. I wandered around the parking lot for what seemed like hours but was probably only twenty or thirty minutes.

Frame after frame, my mind's eye focused slow motion scenes, comparing the Kari in the bed, immobile and unresponsive, with Kari, the irrepressible college-bound senior, who had been such a vibrant focal point of our lives only a few days ago. Pictures of her face emerged and reemerged in my memory. Images of her present, sorry state eclipsed every smiling portrait that crossed my mind

All at once I knew Kari was gone for good. Vivacious, delightful Kari was not going to wake up. Whoever did wake up was going to be a new Kari. And I had the strongest sense the new Kari would bear little resemblance to the person she had been before. I was suddenly enraged: angry at myself, angry at the hospital, angry at the world. If I'd known how, I would have cried. If I could have yelled, I would have screamed, "Kari is gone!"

Just then I saw our friend Ken pull into the parking lot. He is very close to me and our family, and he had driven over to make sure I had some support on Kari's transfer day.

"Do you want me to walk with you for a while?" he asked.

I was curt with him. "I don't want to walk with you or anybody else," I snapped. I turned away abruptly, so distraught I couldn't cope with anyone's company, not even Ken's.

Eventually I made my way back to Kari's room. She was sleeping, and her head was tilted to the left, reenacting her last startled reflex action before the cars collided.

Oh God, I thought, *I wish I could turn back the clock and somehow, some way keep the accident from happening. If only...*

I stared at Kari's limp, sleeping form. Would I ever talk with her again? Or had we already had our last conversation?

Again, my body was assaulted by wave after wave of anger, frustration, and loss. I was all but drowning in pain. Yet strangely, in the midst of that terrible moment a future was born, a new beginning I could not yet foresee. I think it was then and there that I was able to let go of the Kari we'd known and loved for eighteen years, so I could embrace an all-new Kari.

It would be many weeks before the terms "Kari I" and "Kari II" would come into our vocabulary to describe the pre- and post-accident uniqueness of people. But that day, during those agonizing moments, I finally grieved the loss of my beautiful, beloved daughter.

CHAPTER FIVE

On the Move

"Luther, I'm not so sure about this," my wife said, a frown firmly in place between her eyes.

To put it mildly, Kari's first day and night at Daniel Freeman turned out to be troublesome and traumatic for Gin and me. The nurses weren't checking on Kari every five minutes like they had at Harbor. No one seemed particularly interested in her needs or concerned about her condition. Maybe we should have interpreted their easygoing attitude as good news. Maybe we should have been encouraged. But we didn't. And we weren't.

"The nurses take a pretty casual approach around here, don't they?" I responded, glancing at Kari. To my worried eyes, she once again looked as fragile as she had the first night in the surgical recovery room.

Just then, a nurse came in. "It's getting near the end of visiting hours," she pointed out.

"Well, thanks for the reminder, but we'd like to stay a while," I smiled as warmly as possible, taken aback by her unexpected announcement. "At Harbor we kind of got used to sticking around. We don't want Kari to feel alone…"

"I understand. It's a difficult transition for parents," she smiled. "But you'll make it!"

"We'd really like to stay," Gin's voice sounded plaintive. I guess she was pleading a little, to see how that worked.

"I'm sorry," said the nurse, more firmly than before. "It's way past closing time and you need to go home."

"Who's going to watch her?" Gin persisted. "How is anyone going to make sure she doesn't pressure out and damage her brain further?"

"Kari will be fine. I know it's hard the first couple of nights, but she'll be fine. I'm sorry. It's time for you to go."

"I can't bear to leave Kari all alone in a new place," said Gin weakly. I could hear the tears welling up in her voice.

I stood up, moved toward the door, and motioned to Ginger. Like it or not, we had to leave. By then we could only get out through the emergency room. All the other entrances and exits had been locked for hours.

Here we go again, I told myself, *giving Kari up.*

This time we were giving her up to the care of a new, untested staff. They might be medical experts in rehab. But we knew our daughter a lot better than they did.

* * * * *

The next morning Gin and I arrived at Daniel Freeman before 7:00 A.M., relieved to see the day shift swinging into operation. The day before, when we'd admitted Kari, the powers that be had requested we bring in some regular clothing for her. They wanted to see Kari in day clothes instead of hospital gowns. The Daniel Freeman message to the Nussbaum family was unmistakable—it was all about getting on with life, both Kari's life and our life.

As we got acquainted with the personnel that day, we noticed a number of other contrasts. Life at Harbor-UCLA was about survival, and in light of that we had been looking for "the Miracle." At Daniel Freeman the goal was recovery—and a commitment to the long haul. We were going to have to get used to seeing Kari's progress as a marathon, not as a 100-meter sprint. The fear began to grow that she might be like this forever or at least for a very long time. The quick miracle we'd counted on simply wasn't happening.

At Harbor, the nurses had measured progress by the little things Kari did, like opening her eyes or involuntarily moving an arm or a leg—tiny glimpses of hope. At Daniel Freeman, however, the caretakers hardly seemed to notice that a new person had moved into one of the rooms. Even less did they seem to be especially interested in her baby steps, those small but encouraging changes that had kept us all going for weeks.

Maybe we were overreacting, but that first day, we were seriously concerned about Kari's survival, afraid she could die because of the staff's lack of attention. Because it was Saturday, no physical therapy was scheduled. In my view, no one was concerned about keeping her range of motion at its present level. At Harbor, a physical therapist had trained us in ranging Kari every day, to keep her muscle tone. At Daniel Freeman no one seemed the least bit interested in the fact that she was going through the weekend without ranging. Furthermore, the surroundings felt more like an apartment than a hospital—far too casual an environment, in our opinion. Bottom line: No one appeared to be paying the least attention to Kari. How would they know how to meet her needs, not to mention ours?

On the plus side, we were now able to be at her bedside for unlimited hours everyday. On Monday, while sitting in her room, we were stunned to see a physical therapist bring a wheelchair in.

"What in the world are you doing?" I asked with an astonished look.

"Taking Kari to physical therapy. She needs to get started with real therapy. We'll take her down the hall to the mat room and get going. Do you want to come along?"

"Sure," I said, not very sure at all about what I was getting myself into.

The next hour was spent with Susan, the physical therapist, beginning to get Kari's body to reorient itself. When the brain shuts down in response to its injury, the brain and the body lose their interconnectedness. There is not a sense of sitting or standing or trunk control or anything. Every single thing a little child learns for the first time must be relearned for the second time, process by process. The physical therapist's primary job is to help the body and mind reconnect.

That same day, Lynn Butler, Kari's speech therapist and soon to be soul mate, came into the room. "Susan, do you mind if I video Kari? I think it will be a great reference point for all of us down the road."

The question needed no answer and Lynn was soon taping Kari. At first, Kari was sitting up, with Susan sitting behind her to support her body. Kari's eyes were open but they showed no signs of seeing. Her head was still locked, looking severely to the left. Her muscles bulged on the right side of her neck, having been strained by the head locked to the left for a month. It was as if Kari was still locked in dread of the Explorer bearing down on her. Her brain had not let go of its fear.

"Luther, why don't you talk to Kari and get her to look at you. Move to the center so we can try to get her to center her head. She seems to respond to you so well," said Lynn.

I moved to the center and tried to get Kari to look at me. It wouldn't happen. I couldn't get her to do any eye-tracking. I certainly couldn't get her to break her doe-like frozen expression of fear of the car colliding. Her locked neck and her fixed gaze were constant reminders that she was being pulled between this world and the next.

I was exhilarated by seeing her dressed in street clothes, being worked on a mat, out of the bed she had been in for a month. This was the new Kari making a recovery. I fought against seeing the reality of the comatose kid who had no controlled response in any part of her body—arm, leg, eye, hand, or trunk.

To make matters worse, we became aware that Kari's weight was dropping dramatically. At the time of the accident, she had weighed in at about 145 pounds. Now she was down to 120 pounds and losing more every day. Although we joked that she had perfected the U-Turn Diet, Ginger and I were troubled about the fact that Kari's ribs were beginning to be visible.

"Aren't you concerned about her weight loss?" I asked one of the nurses, trying not to sound too pushy.

"You don't need to worry about that," she explained. "A person recovering from a traumatic brain injury consumes massive calories. She'll eventually gain back what she's lost."

At first, Kari had been fed intravenously. As she had improved, a feeding tube had been surgically placed directly into her stomach. Before pumping the food in, a syringe was used to extract liquid out of her stomach, to see if her digestive processes were functioning properly. It was nauseating for Gin and me to watch as the green fluid was drawn up, and yellow dietary liquid was added to it. There were times when the feeding tube lock broke loose and those disgusting-looking fluids flowed out onto Kari and her bed.

Whatever it takes, I told myself. *If this is the way to stabilize her weight, we'll just have to handle it.*

Both Gin and I always sensed that Kari received better care when one of us was present. We saw ourselves as silent advocates for her—even if we didn't say anything, the medical team knew we were watching. So we decided to maintain our vigil, not only to make our presence known to the staff, but also to keep reaching out to Kari, to keep summoning her attention, to keep pulling her back into the conscious world.

Our lives revolved around this supporting role: Wake up. Go to Freeman. Watch therapy. Talk to Kari. Share time with well-wishers. Talk to other families. Leave exhausted. Have dinner. See Kristin. Return phone calls. Go to bed. Wake the next day to the same routine. It became *Groundhog Day*. We were destined to repeat the day over and over until we got it right.

* * * * *

For a few days, we continued to balk at the casual, almost cavalier rehab style at Daniel Freeman. However, before long we began to see that whatever they were doing, it was having a positive impact on Kari. Somehow their strategy was helping her to emerge. Moving her out of bed and into therapy was very different from the warehousing conditions Gin had observed at some of the brain injury "maintenance" centers she had visited. In spite of ourselves, little by little we began to get excited about the program. Casually or not, action was being taken. Things were getting done.

We were even more impressed when we saw how energetic the physical therapy program was. Their tactics were far more aggressive than the simple ranging we'd seen before. Susan, Kari's physical therapist, worked diligently at centering Kari's head in a forward position. Jackie Devries, her occupational therapist, repeatedly sat Kari up on the edge of her bed. The goal was to increase her trunk, head, and neck control while relaxing her legs, hands, and arms. After therapy, Kari was resituated in a wheelchair and rolled back to bed.

Often, the stimulation of therapy caused her to get hot and sweaty, so Gin put a fan beside her to help cool her off. Kari also seemed to like kicking her right leg in an automatic response, as the brain struggled to regain control of the body. In fact she did it so much she kept rubbing an open blister on her heel when she was in bed. One day, she kicked so hard her foot hit the bed rail, her big toenail was broken off, and her toe was bloodied. Somehow, in the process, she had also scraped her left foot on the side and bottom. To protect Kari's feet, the nurses wrapped them in towels, and carefully taped the towels in place.

"At least she's moving around," Gin said to one of the therapists.

"Yes, this phase is referred to as 'agitation' and it is a positive. It shows us she's progressing. However, the damage she's doing to her feet is holding her back. The doctors want to start serial casting her feet, but they can't until her skin is in better shape."

Gin looked puzzled. "What do you mean by serial casting?"

The therapist explained that the term "serial casting" referred to a series of casts that would be placed on Kari's feet, to move them slowly back into the correct position. This would prepare her to walk again, once she was ready to try. We couldn't help but feel encouraged—the therapists were actually envisioning a time when Kari would walk again. Still, the process was slow, and at times it seemed Kari would never get past the most rudimentary improvements.

As Kari entered this phase of agitation, a wonderful thing happened. We had worried when she was in intensive care about not raising her ICP, about touching her too much for fear of doing greater damage. One day, when Lynn came into the room and saw how agitated Kari was, she simply crawled into bed with her, held her, and rocked her. Kari calmed down. Lynn looked at us and said, "Don't be afraid to cuddle her. Crawl into bed and comfort her any time you want." Suddenly, we were given back our daughter to hold.

After each day's therapy, Kari got some rest, but afternoon activities kept everyone else busy. First an orderly had to change the linens on Kari's bed. Then another orderly arrived to vacuum her room. This was a cue for Gin and me to put Kari into a wheelchair and take her out to the halls for a little excursion around the floor. We couldn't help but notice she seemed to relax when it was moving, and as we sat out in the common area, she often fell asleep in her wheelchair.

Once Kari was back in her room, Lynn tried to feed her yogurt, which she spooned into her mouth as slowly as possible. Kari could swallow only the tiniest portion. Even that required enormous effort, which made her so tired that she had to be put back into bed, where she quickly fell asleep again.

After 45 minutes, another session of physical therapy began, this time to range Kari's legs. This rigorous routine gave Kari little restful sleep time during the day, which she seemed to need. We tried to keep things quiet between therapies, but the constant noise of the ward made this extremely difficult.

Gin even did a little therapy of her own one day when she sprayed a Kleenex with Obsession, Kari's favorite fragrance. We saw her nostrils respond a bit, sniffing slightly, and we thought she liked it. This was before either one of us had heard about aromatherapy. It just seemed like a good way to give Kari some contact with the outside world. We left the Kleenex on her pillow overnight.

The next day, we saw Kari moving her lips as if she were trying to make a noise. She seemed to be expending an enormous amount of effort, and her eyelids were blinking frantically. I had to admit that they were blinking randomly, and I longed to see the blinks happen more consistently, so I could be sure she was answering me. In the meantime, Kari was coughing less. We could only hope this indicated there was less mucus in her bronchial system to cough up. Less mucus would mean fewer times Kari would have to bear having her lungs "vacuumed out," a process that was painful for us to watch since it seemed to stress Kari severely.

"I think Kari is beginning to respond to therapy," I tentatively said to Gin one day as we left for home.

"I think she is, Lu. I think we chose the right place."

"God, I sure hope so!" we both said in unison.

* * * * *

Somewhere in my childhood, I remember being told that if we were to see the mound of potatoes we were going to eat during the rest of our lives, we would be so intimidated we would never eat a single potato. My feelings about being "in it for the long haul" with Kari didn't have so much to do with the length of time that would pass during her recovery. That wasn't the mound of potatoes I was staring at. I now knew it was going to be "long." What got to me was that Kari wasn't waking up, no matter how much I wanted her to. I was plagued by one enormous question: *How long will this coma last?*

At one point Ginger and I sat down to have a serious conversation about our desires for Kari's future. We had tried to see some pattern of yeses and nos for her— a blink, a squeeze of the hand, a nod. We both agreed it would be a reasonable goal, just to find a way for her to tell us yes and no. At least that way we could find out by questioning her if she was hungry, sad, or hurting. She could further let us know if she wanted to go to sleep, watch television, listen to music, or go outside. We desperately wanted at least that much, even if no more was to come.

When Kari did appear to move, look at something, or chew ice, I would ask the staff, "Do you still say she's in a coma?"

"Yes," they always answered. "It's just a different level of coma than you've seen before. But it's still a coma."

Gin and I had no idea what the "long" in "long haul" meant, but our calendars were now totally open. Our worst enemy was unrealistic eagerness. When we got ahead of the game, our high hopes turned against us and assaulted us with disappointment. Until we settled into the rhythm of the long haul, our loftiest expectations simply couldn't be realized.

But as days turned to weeks, we couldn't help but notice that the staff at Daniel Freeman was doing everything it could to keep Kari going. The staff was invested in her future, and the investment wasn't nearly as casual as we'd first believed.

Kari and her subtle response to the soap opera "Days of Our Lives" is one example of their professional wisdom. It had been one of Kari's favorite shows prior to the accident. Now, at Freeman, sitting in her wheelchair, she didn't really look at the TV, but it was clear when "Days" was on, Kari was in another world. Her eyes had the vacant stare of a blind person who cannot directionally locate anything. Yet, in an odd way, she was very focused.

She didn't look. She didn't track with her eyes, but she showed us, beyond a shadow of a doubt, she knew when "Days of Our Lives" was on. During the show, she simply would not respond to anything else. The physicians could not examine her and the PTs could not budge her. So finally they just let her watch. Their patience was extraordinary. Who else but a professional team of their caliber would have believed that Kari could relearn trunk control from sitting lazily in her wheelchair watching "Days of Our Lives"?

After a week, one nurse pointed out that, during the drama itself, Kari looked toward the screen intently but during the commercials, she relaxed. For us, this was a wonderfully hopeful sign because it demonstrated some of what the medical team called "range of intensity." That meant her mind was again functioning enough to sort out the difference between the storyline and the commercials.

About a week later, the staff began to notice Kari could track a finger with her eyes, and we noticed she was distracted by a vacuum cleaner outside her room. They were not only amazed at her progress, but they duly recorded it, jotting down every detail.

Gin and I couldn't keep our hopes from soaring. Didn't all this mean that Kari was about to come out of the coma? What else were we to think? The two of us second-guessed ourselves a lot in our evening conversations at home. Were we observing and sensing or were we projecting false hopes? Until we heard her speak to us, we promised each other we weren't going to let ourselves believe she really had emerged into consciousness. Nonetheless, we were certainly energized and inspired by her new attentiveness.

* * * * *

Prior to the accident, Kari had been a thrill-seeker. She had gone bungee jumping in Australia and the two of us had pledged to do a parachute jump after her high school graduation. After we got Kari into a wheelchair, I noticed she retained her love of motion. So that's when I came up with a new plan.

Already the staff was letting me roll Kari around the halls to balance the quiet time—time her mind needed to repair itself—with exposure and stimulation. I reasoned that the more Kari was reminded of the outside world, the better chance she had of making it her destination.

By my nature, I am basically a rule follower. But one Sunday in May, as I moved Kari down the hall, I felt an urge building in me, a longing to take Kari outside and to explore the grounds with her. So I moved quietly toward the door and nudged it open. Then the two of us broke free!

I was sure someone was going to come chasing after me and tell me Kari wasn't ready to be outside and I was putting her at risk. But on weekends supervision was lax. No one seemed to notice.

Once outside, I rolled Kari to the back of the property toward the grass, the trees, and a set of swings. First, I sat down and talked to her for a while. I glanced around furtively from time to time, but still no one appeared to apprehend us. Finally I took a deep breath and headed for my real destination—the small running track that ran around the grounds.

I knew Kari very well, and I was quite convinced that reconnecting her to the outside world would involve speed. I figured I could run Kari around the track and still keep her safely in the chair.

I started out slowly, in a trot.

Kari listed to port with her left arm rubbing against the wheel. I stopped and rearranged her.

After a couple more false starts, I figured out a way for her to remain upright while I jogged. I propped her up in a different position, and that time my strategy worked. I increased our speed and moved into a sprint. I was exhilarated. I was running with my daughter again.

After three laps, I thought I'd better wrap it up. With as little obviously heavy breathing as possible, I rolled her back inside. She immediately fell asleep and stayed that way for about an hour still sitting upright in her chair.

The following Sunday, I took her out again. I was quite sure she enjoyed the activity. But when I was going back into the hospital, I noticed a small burned spot on her left arm, which must have dropped down onto the wheel. The therapists also saw it the next day and were perplexed about what could have possibly caused it. I didn't bother to explain.

Burn or no burn, I believed the stimulation was worth the risks. And my gut feeling was rewarded: the combination of outside exercise and sleep made Kari super-alert for a short period of time afterward. I could feel her increased attentiveness, even though the tangible signs of it were impossible to describe.

* * * * *

At Daniel Freeman, as at Harbor-UCLA, Gin was once again the facilitator, the expediter, and the expert in patient/caretaker relations. For me, being in the hospital was about healing Kari, not about managing the facility. But Gin was gifted. She had quickly learned volumes about how the informal hospital systems work and what it takes to get things done.

When Kari moved to Daniel Freeman, she was given a private room, comfortable but small. It was the second room on the left after entering the ward, and there wasn't much to see out the window. Next to Kari's was a mid-size room, pinkish in tone, with very large windows and much better light. One morning the patient in the mid-sized room moved out, and Ginger immediately scoped out the possibilities. Within minutes Gin was arranging for Kari to be moved into the newly vacated room.

The nurses put up a predictable amount of resistance, but Gin would not have any of it. She even got one of the therapists to help her pack Kari's clothes and roll her chair right into the new room.

Done! She congratulated herself, unable to repress a smile. *Possession is nine-tenths of the law.* Kari was now in a much larger and brighter space, with trees outside the window and sunlight warmly streaming across her bed.

With more space available, we began to bring in things we thought Kari would enjoy: a stereo, a VCR with tapes she loved, which we played over and over—*Dirty Dancing, Ghost,* and *Pretty Woman.* We posted a large homemade calendar, a poster where dozens of her friends wrote notes of encouragement, and countless photos of friends and family, which we made into a collage. Gin made sure there were always fresh flowers on display. Once we even smuggled in a kitten, which stimulated some of Kari's first hand movements.

In this new, friendlier setting, Kari even got better baths. Previously, she had been bathed in what I called a "human car wash." The nurses had put Kari, naked, on a trolley cart with fold-up plastic sides and wheeled her down the hall to the shower room. There, they washed her down like a mud-spattered Chevy. It was primitive, but successful and she emerged clean—hair and all. Now, however, she could be showered while sitting in her wheelchair, a process that afforded more privacy and warmth. And, to my relief, a great deal more dignity. A nurse we nicknamed Attila the Hun soaped her hair and hurried her through the shower so fast that soap would painfully sting her eyes. Though Kari could not speak to complain about it, she soon seemed to dread even those showers.

* * * * *

About this time, a group of research people came over from Harbor-UCLA to see Kari for her first follow-up study. They were accumulating data on recovery rates for Emergency Room patients, and when they saw Kari's progress at Freeman, they were amazed. That's when we were painfully reminded that in the ER Kari's eyes had been fixed and dilated. The pupils had not responded to light. The researcher observed that it was extremely rare for anyone not responding to light to survive, and even more unusual to achieve any amount of recovery. Kari's case was a statistical miracle. Again, we were inspired to continue. In all our blind optimism, we had been right from the beginning. We weren't about to stop trying now.

* * * * *

Newly motivated, I began to wheel Kari around inside the hospital, looking for new places to explore. On the second floor, outside the rehab ward, was the stroke ward. The spinal injury ward was off to the left. For obvious reasons, there wasn't much going on there. To the right was a long hall, and at the end of that another ward, and then a bridge, which passed over a driveway. I decided to see what was across the bridge, so off we went.

From the bridge, I could see and hear airplanes making their final approach into LAX. I tried to get Kari to connect with airplanes and travel. "Look, Kari!" I told her. "Those people are coming in from Europe or Australia. Remember your trip to Australia? Do you remember?"

She was impassive, but I kept trying. How I longed to see her respond!

At the end of the bridge was a chapel. In my youth, I had spent a lot of time in churches, and I was drawn into this little sanctuary.

As I wheeled Kari inside, I recalled my early years, attending Presbyterian churches. My father's family was Evangelical Mennonite, and one of my uncles was a minister in that denomination. My mom's dad was a Lutheran minister. I have Amish ancestors a couple of generations back. As a young man, I was once very involved in the church, even to the point of being selected to give two sermons on Youth Sundays.

Somewhere along the way, I became discouraged with organized religion. But as the two of us entered the chapel, I walked inside acknowledging that the principles and values of Christianity continued to provide a great guide for my life and my family. Over the years, I'd had a few transformative moments in churches. And looking back, I guess what happened inside the chapel at Daniel Freeman turned out to be another one.

The chapel there is very small, three pews with an aisle down the middle. Because Daniel Freeman is a part of the Catholic hospital system, the chapel had the traditional trappings of any Catholic chapel, but I wasn't looking at them. I was in the moment with my daughter, in search of something—anything—that would help her reconnect her with the world; something that would touch her emotions. Then it struck me. What could be more emotional to a young girl than the thought of her own wedding?

Before I knew it, I was describing an exquisite daydream to Kari as I walked her down the aisle.

"Look," I whispered, "there's the groom, up there on the right. And his best man is standing there, right next to him." I paused to give her time to process what I was saying.

"And there's your maid of honor," I continued, "on the left. Oh, Kari, they're starting the music. Let's go. Here comes the bride, all dressed in white."

I sang the wedding march as our little procession moved slowly down the aisle.

Who knows what she was thinking? Maybe it meant more to me than it did to her. Maybe not. But it was something I repeated again and again in the course of our hospital walks.

Many fathers walk their daughters down the aisle, but most of them don't sing as they go. I did both. It was, at that time of our lives, an inspiration. I wasn't rehearsing for a future that I knew could never happen. I was simply looking for emotion that could break Kari's long silence.

CHAPTER SIX

The Sweetest Words

Gin and I required ourselves to learn all we could about the recovery process Kari was going through. And once we first heard about serial casting, we realized we had a whole new set of lessons to learn. Some of those lessons turned out to be simply factual. Others were emotionally painful for us and physically agonizing for Kari.

When the brain is injured, the body shifts into a radical defensive mode. Most now believe the brain grabs all the calories available for the massive repairs it needs to make. Limbs shut down and curl up. When arms and legs have been in defensive posture for a long time—in a posture similar to the fetal position—tendons lengthen on one side and shorten on the other.

Calcium, sent in to help make repairs, gets stuck in the clumped muscles and creates deposits. One way to prevent buildup and recover range of motion is to put the limbs in a cast. Casts "set" them in the right position again. Through the process of serial casting, doctors and therapists try to force the body to realign itself properly.

Of all the events along the road back, Kari's "casting parties" were the worst. The staff arrived and went to work by taking up positions on either side of her, often joining her in bed. They pushed on her foot, for example, as hard as they could to get it to relax a little bit and to stretch out. Therapists then held the foot in position while the doctors applied a cast to it. After several days, the same team took the old cast off, forced a little additional range out of her foot, and then recast it.

In the case of Kari's foot, the stress was compounded by the blister on her right heel, which had first appeared because of her relentless kicking and had never healed properly. Her wearing of high-top shoes, meant to prevent her feet from "dropping" to a clumped position, had further exacerbated the blister. By now it was an ugly ulcer, with raw flesh exposed almost to the tendon.

Coaxing a muscle-tight limb is excruciating work. In Kari's case it was even more difficult. One of the trials we had enrolled Kari in that first night was a drug in the steroid family. It was a double-blind study. However, within a couple of weeks, we knew she had been given the drug since she grew dark hairs and showed incredible muscle strength. While the steroid helped enormously in keeping her intracranial pressure down, it provided dramatically increased resistance to the casting process.

The casting team called the coaxing process "cranking" because they had to push so hard. They were physically overpowering Kari, fighting against the enhanced condition of her taut muscles, and using all their strength to get the limb to budge only the slightest bit. Even Kari, still comatose, was pushed to the breaking point.

The grimaces of pain on her face were unmistakable. Although she could not speak, Kari's tortured eyes spoke for her. We had to ignore it, but both Gin and I felt like screaming on her behalf, using our voices in place of her silent one. During the sessions, Gin often ran out in tears, while I was asked to help encourage Kari. This was based on my demonstrated ability to reach her and strongly motivate her in some subliminal way.

In the end, the process was less than satisfactory. After four weeks of continuous pain, the doctors measured Kari's muscles and found that in many places they had no measurable gain. The casting simply hadn't worked.

"We'll have to correct some of the imbalances surgically," the doctor told me somewhat apologetically. "But that's not going to happen for a long time. Probably not for months."

"Why didn't it work? What were the odds?"

He looked at me as if I should know by now that everything we were doing for Kari was a gamble. "We win a few and we lose a few," he said with a shrug.

"Well, we can't give up on Kari," I reminded him.

"We aren't going to give up," he agreed as he picked up her files and walked out.

* * * * *

The medical team may have been, like us, committed for the long haul. But that clearly wasn't the case with our insurance provider. Fifty days after the accident, our insurance challenges finally hit full force.

Though I had left my company in December, my compensation had continued through March 31. The accident had occurred on April 2, and during the first hours of Kari's treatment, I had felt a surge of panic, wondering whether or not I had elected COBRA (continuation of benefits) coverage for our family. I simply couldn't remember. Now, weeks later, I finally got a phone call confirming that I had several months after the March 31 termination date to elect COBRA coverage. With a sigh of relief, I immediately made the election, continued our coverage, and eliminated that particular threat. But there was plenty more to worry about.

The next question was, "To what degree are we covered?"

The company I had been with—a company for which I'd served as CEO for three highly successful years—had been sold, and the new parent company had changed the plan in the midst of our ordeal. I was furious they would try to do such a thing. Kari was making such awesome progress I did not want to see it slowed one bit.

Needless to say, some rather intense discussions took place between the company's human resources vice president and me. They were, in fact, more than discussions. They were angry shouting matches. Ultimately, the company bowed to our situation and agreed to maintain the current level of coverage for Kari. But it wouldn't have happened without a fight.

And even that didn't end the uncertainty. Although the new parent corporation was now on board, the insurance company often continuously rattled the saber: If we could not prove Kari was making progress in a defined clinical way, they would not continue to pay for therapy. For them it was simple economics: No visible progress, terminate the expense. A pause in Kari's progress of a few weeks would result in the suspension of therapy.

Once we really understood the process our hearts sank. Weekly, we saw other patients leaving Daniel Freeman because their coverage had run out. Being there long hours during the day, we knew there had been a great deal of progress in the others. How were we going to avoid a similar fate?

We were informed, in no uncertain terms, that elaborate progress reports had to be generated on a regular basis. The rehabilitation team and the supervising neurologist were required to write down in specific detail anything and everything they saw. None of our parental intuitions would make the least difference. If documented progress weren't apparent, rehab would be cut off. It was as simple as that.

The Daniel Freeman team always described Kari as a star patient. At least half of the therapists were genuinely invested in her as a person, caring for her as far more than "just an-other patient." They were also professionals who adhered to high ethical standards. I appreciated that. But the reports they produced were so abstract and dehumanizing, it was hard to catch even a glimpse of hope in their jargon-laden texts.

For example, one week they wrote the following:

> *Eye: three observations of moving eyes to the right with a blank stare. Tracked finger running down nose. Has an apparent 12–18" focal range. Can track motion further away. Head: Moves head to mid-line when sleeping on right side or back. Moved head back to pillow when she lifted up from the chair on command. Attempts to move head to the right. Slight ability to move. Hands: Extreme pained expression on gentle opening of left hand. Lesser pained expression on right hand. Agitation: Very relaxed with motion. Took outside and moved around Sat. and Sun. Very agitated late Sat. and Sunday. Hearing: Appears strong. Is distracted by noise in the common area—vacuum cleaner, friends laugh, etc. Attentiveness: Has fewer periods of good response to questions.*

Kari's progress was monitored in monthly meetings held in a cramped hospital conference room. The chairperson was a case manager whose job was to sell the clinical record taken from the therapists to the insurance company. Those insur-ance meetings were killers for Ginger and me. While we saw enormous progress, we were concerned the therapists or the insurance company would reject our views as nothing more than the wishful thinking of well-meaning parents. It was entirely up to the case manager to make the decision. We felt—and were—powerless.

During the meetings, the medical staff discussed Kari in clinical terms, describing all aspects of her progress, however minute. Meanwhile, the case manager lowered our expectations and expressed ceaseless doubts about her ability to continue to get insurance approvals. *What's wrong with a little hope!* I wondered. Invariably, we felt like we'd taken a body blow when she announced that yes, she had received approval for another two weeks, but no, unless Kari made substantially more progress our benefits would not continue.

Every month I was convinced the insurance company would either cut back Kari's therapy or stop it entirely. That fear was underscored, to our dismay, when week after week we continued to see patients who had come to the hospital at the same time as Kari— some of them even later—disappear. They were gone for one reason—their insurance had run out.

The injustice of the system was outrageous. Brain injuries require both therapy and time to make any significant recovery. It certainly is not a linear recovery process. How dare any insurance bureaucrats inhibit Kari's—or anyone else's—recovery? We entered every meeting in fear and trembling. We left every meeting with a kind of ambivalent elation. We'd managed to keep the benefits going for a two more weeks, but soon there would be yet another review. The possibility of being completely cut off was always just around the corner. The stress on Gin and me was unreal.

Meanwhile, it seemed that all kinds of other things were suddenly going wrong. To begin with, Kari had developed a urinary tract infection, so her permanently inserted Foley catheter had to be removed. Instead, she had to be catheterized with a temporary tube, which was inserted and withdrawn every four hours. That in turn caused Kari's skin to break down, so the medical team decided to retry the Foley.

Along with this, Kari was having too many bowel movements, taxing her energy considerably.

But to top it all off, one of the nurses said, "I'm not sure, but I think Kari had a seizure last night." We were horrified. Nothing of this sort had happened, despite the entire brain trauma. What effect would a seizure have on the insurance caseworker's report? More specifically, how seriously would it jeopardize Kari's recovery?

As it turned out, the nurse was wrong. After checking the symptoms with a doctor, who ran some quick tests, everyone decided it was a false alarm. Thankfully, whatever Kari had was not a seizure. It turned out, instead, just to be another wild, emotional ride for her parents.

We struggled with other glitches as well. Kari's schedule was posted on a master board in the main hall. We couldn't help but notice that the schedule was not always adhered to.

Then there were the substitute therapists. Nothing was clearer to us than that therapy was all about relationships. Even when Kari was in a coma, we could sense a different response from her to the people she liked and she didn't like. The substitute physical therapists were mechanical, and mechanical doesn't work for therapy. Kari went backward on the days when subs were working. She didn't cooperate; she didn't allow her muscles to relax.

One particular sub didn't seem to have the slightest idea how to work with her. "What should I do now?" she'd ask, looking worried and puzzled. Gin and I tried to show her what we knew, but we were always disappointed when she showed up. Kari reacted so well when talented therapists worked with her. Why waste time with those who weren't?

One of the most gifted people ever to work with Kari was Waleed A'boudi, the director of therapy and a noted lecturer. From time to time he conducted Kari's therapy himself. His interaction with her was nothing short of a ballet. With the room extremely quiet, he sat behind Kari and began to move her gently, gracefully, sensing from her how far she was able to bend.

Many other therapists had a preset routine in mind. If Kari gave them unconscious resistance, they tried to push through it. This man never seemed to encounter resistance, taking full advantage of his own well-honed intuition and Kari's natural motion and responses.

Even though we were very experienced observers of therapy, with the subs, we had to learn to be diplomatic, careful not to let our dominant, type-A personalities try to take over the running of the program. To run a marathon, you don't count the miles; you concentrate on establishing a rhythm. The rhythm is self-reinforcing, while the mind's need for milestones is its own worst enemy. We tried our best to pace ourselves by simply avoiding milestones, and instead noting Kari's progress, briefly applauding it, then moving forward without looking back.

* * * * *

One morning Lynn, the speech therapist who seemed to have a special sensitivity for Kari, concluded that she was ready to have her tracheotomy tube taken out. With this tube out, we heard Kari's breathing make sounds, a cross between natural gurgles and purposeful grunts. Was she trying to speak to us? Time would tell. It was also Lynn who noticed Kari might be ready for her first solid food. Next thing we knew, she was spoon-feeding Kari little bites of Jell-O.

Gin wrote in her journal around this time:

> Kari's body is working on a new thing with her right leg, "marching" in bed, a great aerobic exercise! And in therapy, her tummy crunches are now almost full sit-ups; she's recovering that much flexibility in her trunk.
>
> And Kari's new "positioning" wheelchair arrived today, thanks to our friend Dick Chandler. Kari took right to it, doing better with her head by leaning it forward and bringing it back to the chair. Her trunk control is good in the chair and was also better when on the mat, holding

herself up for three to four seconds, with the therapist's help, of course, but always increasing muscle tone and having it documented!

* * * * *

Ginger and I didn't "go" to Daniel Freeman, we "camped" there. It was a 45-minute drive from our house in Palos Verdes, so once we got there, we stayed, arriving early in the morning and leaving late in the day. Ginger and I would overlap our visits. I arrived at seven and left at four; Ginger came in at eleven and left around eight.

As weeks turned to months and June approached, I began to dream about Kari being wheeled across the stage to receive her high school diploma. The ceremony at Peninsula High School in Palos Verdes is conducted outdoors on the football field, with more than a thousand graduating seniors. In my mind I saw myself wheeling Kari up the ramp and pushing her across the stage toward the podium and the principal. The crowd was standing and the applause was building to a thunderous crescendo. Kari was back!

Before the accident, I had felt blasé about Kari's high school graduation, looking forward instead to college and graduate school—the ones that counted. But after the accident, the importance of her high school graduation was quickly magnified. Peninsula High School had notified us that Kari had already earned enough credits for graduation. And, because of all her friends and ours, even when it was clear that Kari could not join us, Ginger and I had planned on attending.

But as we drove away from Freeman on graduation day toward Palos Verdes, we weren't comfortable. Both of us were starting to dread the evening's events.

"I don't know, Gin," I said. "Something doesn't feel right."

"You wanted to go to graduation, didn't you?"

"I know," I said, "but it just doesn't feel right."

"You mean going without Kari?"

"Yeah," I said. "It really doesn't make sense."

"You know," said Gin, "maybe we made plans for this without thinking about how we would feel about it. I know I wanted to be there for all her friends but I didn't think enough about how I would really feel, being there without Kari."

"What do you want to do?" I asked.

"I don't know. Anyway, we're almost there." We were driving up Hawthorne Boulevard, a few blocks shy of the campus.

Just then Gin said, "Look, we're by Misto's. Why don't we go in and have dinner? After all, we're early. Maybe we'll feel more like going after we eat."

We found a table on the patio and each ordered a glass of wine.

It occurred to me that with all of the hospital commuting, Gin and I hadn't had much time for just the two of us. We'd taken virtually no time off for ourselves. We had been fabulous parents and caretakers, but there hadn't been much energy for the conversation and intimacy that makes a couple. Now, at Misto's, we were enjoying each other's company, having a relaxed intimate time. We began to talk about Kari's future.

Shortly after the accident, I had done a review of her status with the colleges she had applied to. One of those, the University of Colorado at Boulder, had already returned her acceptance. I had requested that they defer her admission for a year. "She's had a little accident," I explained, "and probably won't be ready to attend college in the fall of 1993." That gave her an extra year from her scheduled start. I had honestly thought that she might be ready by then.

"Things certainly look different now, don't they?" Gin remarked.

"It seems that no matter what goals I set, I have to constantly revise them. I always have to refocus on more realistic plans. I guess some of my ideas are just a little too aggressive."

"Your goals may sometimes be a little bit ahead of the game," Gin smiled, "but they always get everyone moving in the right direction."

"It's funny. On the one hand it was hard on me to postpone college for Kari," I admitted. "But on the other, compared to the victory of Kari watching 'Days of Our Lives,' college doesn't seem like it means much after all."

"It's important for us to celebrate the little things Kari accomplishes. Little things lead to big things."

We sat quietly for a while.

Then Gin asked me, "Do you feel depressed, Lu, that your dream for Kari isn't coming true?"

"What do you mean?" I protested. "Kari is making huge progress!"

"A lot of your dreams for her have been shattered. It would be normal to feel down."

"I don't know," I said. "I don't like to feel down. Sometimes I feel disappointed but then the next day, I wake up with a new vision. Kari II is making unbelievable progress!"

"It's been such an intense couple of months, Lu."

There was a pause.

"So what are we going to do about graduation?"

There was another brief silence, while both of us sipped our wine.

"A lot of people will be looking for us. I feel guilty about not going," Gin finally replied.

"I know, but the truth is, I don't want to be with several thousand other people right now," I told her. "It just feels good to sit here with you."

Our eyes met. We felt comfort in each other. Without another word, we both acknowledged that Peninsula High

School's graduation that year was not a celebration for us. It was an important event for thousands of other people, but not for the Nussbaums. We ordered another glass of wine, a couple of entrees, and stayed put.

As we relaxed on Misto's patio, in the distance, we could hear the sounds of the ceremony, the graduation march, and the applause. We knew there would be a moment of silence to recognize Kari, the graduating classmate in the hospital. We were glad we weren't there. How could we have explained that their silence was in honor of Kari I, while we had come to know and love someone we now called Kari II? Our hearts were unconditionally with her.

The peace Gin and I shared that night was as warm and embracing as the June ocean breeze. Again, we had let go of something old. In exchange, we had received something new—an acceptance of Kari's new life and a genuine delight with our role in it.

* * * * *

With Kari continuing to progress, Kristin was able to get away for the first time, traveling to Minneapolis to attend a Spanish language camp and then down to San Diego to be a part of Supercamp. Although the language camp was fun and low key, Supercamp was a significant experience for Kristin. Supercamp provides teenagers with a number of tools for speed reading, memory retention, and grade maximization. However, its main goal is to create an extremely supportive environment where the kids can help each other grow in a myriad of ways. Kristin found a receptive, supportive group where she could verbalize her trauma of the past year.

The last day of the camp, parents were invited to participate with their kids in a final ceremony, which involved the breaking of a 1-inch-thick pine board with bare hands. Each person was asked to write the problems he or she wanted to conquer on the board. Everyone agreed no one would leave until all the boards were broken! Kristin wrote, "Kari. Recovery." on her board. It was fabulous to be there to watch Kris apply her newly learned mind-focus techniques to break through the board. Maybe Kari could recover.

* * * * *

The day after graduation, Kari was very tired. She just wanted to sleep and be left alone by everyone. Even though two therapists were recasting her arm and hand, stretching them relentlessly into new positions, Kari was calm and quiet. In fact, she slept through it all. I wondered if the peace Ginger and I had experienced the previous night at dinner had somehow been mysteriously passed on to Kari.

Later that week, Kari perked up again, demonstrating renewed awareness of her surroundings. In physical therapy, she moved her left leg and rolled around on the mat, on command, to the right and to the left.

Previously, she had kept her tongue on the roof of her mouth. Now she took ice into her mouth and used her tongue to move it around.

An all-important question lingered around us like a sweet fragrance, like a scent of hope: Would Kari be able to vocalize soon? Were tongue movements related to her eye movements? Surely they must be.

Previously, Kari's eyes had looked only to the left. Now, she kept her head up when sitting in her wheelchair, while her eyes moved from left to right, following a nurse's footsteps across the room. I reflected back on that magic day when Kari's fixed, frightened stare to the left had finally been broken, and her head had moved back to the center. Each of the therapists had worked for days to gently coax Kari out of the frozen left position. While helping in therapy, I had reached to Kari's eye and removed a piece of "sleep" from the corner of her right eye. The pressure of my finger in exactly that spot suddenly caused Kari to move her head to the center for the first time since the accident. Such a little thing, yet such a major event to unlock more recovery.

* * * * *

Every day since the accident, we had looked for, hoped for, reached for our minimal communicative interaction with Kari—a clear wink, a hand squeeze, a recognizable sound—any tangible sign. For eighty-two days, we received no substantial signal. We had seen things we thought *might* be responses, but they were inconsistent. So we could only conclude no communication had yet taken place.

Then came day eighty-three.

Gin had been on hospital duty that morning. I had gone to a business meeting. Kari's room was directly opposite the door to the ward, with electronically controlled doors that prevented brain-injured patients from wandering into the hospital. After walking through that door, it was probably twenty steps across the common area to enter Kari's private room. As I hurried into the hospital after my meeting, I saw Gin a few steps outside Kari's room. She had gone to lunch and was coming back just before one o'clock at the end of "Days of Our Lives." I was no more than ten steps behind her.

As we went into Kari's room and stopped at her bedside, as she always did, Gin said, "Hi, Kari."

I saw Kari turn her head away from the TV, look at Gin, focus clearly, and say, "Hi…hi, hi, hi."

My heart caught in my throat.

I stepped around Ginger so Kari could see me.

"Hi," she said to me, too. Then she gave me her first smile!

Gin and I were stunned. We could hardly believe what we had heard, but this time the vocalizations were unmistakable.

To say that I was ecstatic is an understatement. A baby's first words are expected, but we had no assurance Kari II would ever speak at all. A warm wave of amazement and success swept over me. All our efforts had paid off, and this was our reward. I felt triumphant and moved to tears and astonished and weak in the knees, all at the same time.

We called out to the nurses in the hall and Jackie, Kari's occupational therapist, came running in at once.

"Hi," Kari said to her.

Dr. Begozian walked in too.

"Hi," Kari repeated.

All of us were cheering and grinning and crying at the same time.

"Kari's out of her coma!" I exclaimed, feeling somehow vindicated in the eyes of the doctor.

"Yes, she's out," he laughed. "Congratulations!"

We called Kristin, who was off at camp. She was so excited by the news that she asked me to put the phone to Kari's ear.

Kari said, "Hi" to her sister over the phone. Then she clammed up for the rest of the day, having worn herself out with all the effort. She drifted back to sleep with a sweet, peaceful look on her face.

But there was more.

Four days later, I had early duty, getting Kari ready for therapy. But we didn't make it to therapy that morning. Kari was in her wheelchair about 10:50 and was looking all around. I felt so very happy just to be with her, to see her aware and somewhat alert. I carried a chair over next to her and placed it so I could lean forward and give her a hug.

Kari and I embraced, which we had done before. But this time she wouldn't let go. Never since the accident had I seen in her so much intent, so much muscle control. Kari just held on and held on. Then she began to sob. Her tear ducts didn't yet work, but Kari's deepest feelings bubbled to the surface and poured out.

We held each other so long that my back began to hurt. I adjusted myself and sat up straight. Feeling profoundly connected to her, I looked into my daughter's eyes and said, "Kari, I really love you."

She was looking directly at me when she answered. "I...love...you...too," she said.

The words came out broken and slowly, but they were clear and distinct.

Kari had spoken. She had formed an entire sentence. And the words she had chosen were the sweetest words she has ever said to me.

I cried with joy and relief. Together Kari and I hugged and sobbed for what seemed like an hour.

When Kris and Gin arrived around 11:45, Kari also said "Hi," to them, and "I love you." It brought all of us to tears. At last our whole family was back together, for the first time in months. None of us could stop crying.

Throughout the hospital ordeal, I had invested my time, my ideas, my efforts, my life, with no real expectation or assurance of any outcome. Now I had received the fruit of my labor. How many eighteen-year-old daughters are willing to openly express their love for their fathers? Kari was and Kari did. Maybe we had to go through the worst kind of tragedy to appreciate the depth of our relationship. But her honest, simple words were worth it all. They meant everything to me.

That night I didn't drive home, I flew.

I couldn't have touched the road if I'd tried.

I was the happiest man alive.

CHAPTER SEVEN

On the Road Again

The first exciting days after Kari's awakening passed quickly, and life soon settled down to a pattern of more hard work, more tedious repetition, and more patience. We received wonderful news as the brain swelling decreased and the CAT scans showed only visible damage to the left occipital lobe. This is the center for sight and we discovered over time that Kari could not see anything that was low or to the right. She had acquired stroke-type damage because of the oxygen starvation caused by the hematoma.

At eighteen years old, Kari had to relearn almost all of her basic developmental functions. She was unable to sit up by herself, get out of bed, go to the bathroom, shower, brush her hair or teeth, or even feed herself. And we were soon to become acquainted with the word for Kari's most hated disability: aphasia. It wasn't easy, but breakthroughs in her recovery made the effort seem worthwhile. By now, at least she understood us when we spoke to her. And now she was able to respond to us with the yes or no we so much looked forward to hearing.

"Do you want to go outside for a while?" Gin would inquire.

"Yes," Kari would respond.

"Are you hungry?" I'd ask.

"No," she'd say.

Occasionally she would mimic parts of sentences. For example, one afternoon before I walked over to the nurse's station to get a glass of ice, I said, "Ice, okay?"

She smiled and answered, "Okay."

She hadn't said okay before, and I was delighted to hear it. But Kari was still having trouble originating language. Words were hard to find. Ginger came in later that afternoon and asked, "How are you, today?"

Kari replied in a series of mumbles that made no sense whatsoever. I felt a surge of disappointment. I so wanted Kari to communicate her needs and feelings to us, and to begin to initiate conversation. The therapists began to acquaint us with more about the medical condition "aphasia." With aphasia, the patient has word-finding problems. Some cannot understand words when they hear them, some cannot find the word they want to say, others have both problems. It seemed that Kari only had trouble with finding the word. This meant she could understand everything that was said to her, but speaking, for her, was like needing to say what you want in a completely foreign language. We began to understand this by testing Kari ourselves.

"Kari, what is this?" we would ask as we pointed to an object such as a chair. She would look at it and then us with a puzzled look.

"Kari, would you please point to the bed?" we would ask and were delighted when she was able to consistently point to the object we asked her about. Though we knew this would be a tremendous frustration for our once-exceptionally verbal daughter who had aspired to be a reporter or a writer, we were relieved she was able to at least understand what was said. We later were to discover that aphasia extended to reading and writing as well. Later, in a Santa Monica College paper she wrote, Kari described her aphasia in this way:

"I awoke from a three-month coma and found myself completely unable to find a word in my brain, let alone get one out of my mouth. It was like trying to sing my favorite song but forgetting all the lyrics....My aphasia is most closely related to Broca's aphasia, which occurs when there is damage to the frontal lobe of the brain. This 'non-fluent aphasia is generally characterized by an effortful, hesitant, telegraphic style of speech marked by pauses. Speech is low and sentences are frequently incomplete' (Fact Sheet). In addition, 'people with these symptoms often have right-sided weakness or paralysis of the arm and leg because the frontal lobe is also important for body movement' (Loss of Speech). In my case, I lost quite a bit of strength and ability in my right arm and leg. Difficulties with grammar and vocabulary appear both in speaking and in writing.

"Though individuals with non-fluent aphasia have trouble talking, they usually have a good understanding of speech....The four months of not being able to talk seemed like a lifetime of torture. I felt like I was a mummy who was waking up for the first time. Before my accident, reading, writing and talking were my strongest skills. I loved being able to debate issues and thoughts with my family and friends. Now, I feel like I have been robbed of that luxury. The aphasia is not only hard on me, but on my family and friends as well....I still feel depressed when I am talking and people do not look at me, or ignore me. I feel even more bothered by lack of ability to communicate my thoughts. In my mind, I can carry out a good conversation and often carry on an argument with myself, but when it comes to talking out loud, I have problems.;"

The therapists were hopeful Kari's communication skills would improve, but they cautioned us there was a possibility they might not. One of the most humorous sides of her apha-sia as it improved was the running together of her terms for Gin and me. She called us both "momdad."

Aphasia was the main limiting factor as Kari sought to reenter and merge with the mainstream. Along the way, she called for a pizza. "I, I, I wud (slurred) li, li, like a a a peproni (slurred) pizza…." The telephone order person interrupted, "Don't call here again. We don't have to take orders from drunks." Phone slammed down.

In spite of these setbacks, as time went on we couldn't help but notice little signs of progress—including another one that was amusing. Although Kari was not talking very well, she had taken up winking. And she was witty about it. Some-times she responded to an obvious "no" question with a "yes," and then winked at the speaker and laughed or said, "Yeah, yeah, yeah." And if a guy she liked happened to be in the room, she'd add a kiss to the wink.

As I watched these things happen, I thought of them as signs of life. It was new, healthy growth, a little unruly and awkward at times, but growth just the same. It did my heart good.

* * * * *

The slowest of Kari's systems to come back to normal were her arms and hands. She could wipe her nose. She could scratch her legs. She could feed herself toast and sandwiches. But her fingers were still very stiff, and she sometimes lost control and accidentally scratched herself or dropped a sand-wich. More than once lettuce, tomato, and mayonnaise spilled down her t-shirt, leaving a pattern of scattered stains.

To assist with her hand development, the staff fitted Kari with arm and hand splints to be worn all night and during various parts of the day. With each passing week, her range of motion increased and she needed the splints less and less.

Her right arm was the tightest, injured from the calcium formation.

Tests had revealed that during her post-accident recuperation period, Kari's brain had dispatched an enormous amount of calcium to her right elbow. Drs. Ludwig and Begozian told me it could be removed by surgery "but we'll have to wait a year to make sure the brain has stopped sending the calcium there."

"A year?" I exclaimed, watching Kari's painful effort to use her arm.

"There's no point in doing it twice," he explained. "We've got to deal with her legs first, in any case."

"What's going on with her legs, anyway? They seem so stiff and never seem to straighten out all the way. Is this due to the intense tone, the defensive posture her body had been locked in?"

He nodded. "Yes. The biggest problem is with her Achilles tendons. They've shortened to the point that regular physical therapy can't stretch them back long enough. That's why it's impossible for Kari to stand up with her legs straight. To get straight legs, we have to go in and lengthen the Achilles tendons as well as the hamstring muscles."

We scheduled the surgery, based on this diagnosis. Everyone agreed there was no alternative. Gin and I submitted to the medical team without much discussion.

The day before surgery one of the doctors stopped by to see her. "Well, Kari," he grinned, "tomorrow's the big day! Are you ready?"

"Yes."

"Good," he said. "I've just got a few forms here for your parents to look over."

He handed Gin some documents before he left. "If you have questions we can talk more in my office," he remarked casually.

Gin read the papers while I sat with Kari. As I looked into Kari's eyes, I could see she was ready for surgery. She had regained some of her old strength and courage, and it was evident in her demeanor.

But after a minute or two of quiet reading, Gin came over and whispered to me quietly, "Lu, this form scares the hell out of me."

"Isn't it just the usual stuff, protecting the hospital from malpractice liabilities?"

"It's not just that," she shook her head. "I think you'd better have a look."

I took the form outside and began to go through it line by line. Gin gave me a few minutes and then came outside.

"My God!" I said, looking up at her. "I didn't realize that so many things could go wrong if you put a brain-injured patient under general anesthesia."

"Neither did I. You know, I'm not so sure about this surgery. We've just come through three months of fighting to bring Kari back to life. She's awake and speaking now. I don't think I could handle it if anything went wrong. Is this worth the risks?"

We sat quietly for a minute or two. "I don't want to give up any ground we've gained either," I said slowly. "It's true there are some serious risks involved if we go ahead with the surgery. But what about the risks if we don't?"

"What do you mean?" Gin frowned.

"Not taking this risk might condemn Kari to a wheelchair."

Another silence fell between us.

Gin sighed deeply. "You're right."

"I guess we pretty much have to go for it, don't we?"

Gin looked at me with tears in her eyes. "Why does everything have to be so hard?"

Kari had surgery at 11:00 A.M. the next day. To say the least, we were terrified. We didn't say much to each other. We tried to deal with our worst fears privately. There was no point in talking about them. But we knew when we looked into each other's eyes what the other was probably thinking. Our hands reached out to one another.

Of course we were waiting in the recovery room when the doctor came in.

We searched his face, but this time it was neither grave nor detached. "Everything went just fine. No problem at all," he announced with a big smile.

An hour later Kari rolled in, zonked out, with a full cast on her right leg, up onto her thigh, and a half cast on the left leg up to her knee. Her legs and arms were now both in the corrected position—with casts on her legs and splints on her arms. Time would tell the tale.

Kari spent the next week or two in bed, quietly mending. She was receiving Demerol for the pain and was tolerating it well, though it left her a bit spacey. With her legs cast, she couldn't roll around in her wheelchair, anyway. When she was not sleeping, she answered questions thickly and was easily confused. For the time being, the teasing winks had ceased.

In a week, the doctors changed Kari's casts to check the stitches, and in doing so they made a great discovery: Her right leg was in such good shape they were able to substitute a knee cast for the full leg cast. That meant all sorts of good things. Kari was again able to use her wheelchair, she sat up more easily while getting dressed, and before long, she had regained enough trunk control to kneel on the workout mat.

Progress was resumed and with the surgery behind us, the future once again looked bright. It had been worth the risk.

Three weeks later, Kari got a chance to use her new legs. As usual, the physical therapists on the morning shift took her down to the therapy room. Since her hands were not yet strong enough to hold her up, she was placed in a walker designed so she could support herself by resting on her forearms.

And at long last, with the help of that walker, Kari II took her first steps: awkward and tentative and strongly supported, but steps, real steps. I was amazed by how quickly her brain remembered what her legs were supposed to do. We could see the pain on her face as she struggled with her muscles, and eventually she grew tired and gave up. But Kari was acting like her old diligent and determined self, and asked for an afternoon session to give it another go.

A few days later, as the afternoon session was starting with leg exercises to warm up her muscles, an idea popped into my mind. Many years before in an effort to have Kari give up sucking her thumb, I had made a bet with her. If she would quit sucking her thumb I had offered to pay her $25. That thumb was never in her mouth again. Remembering this I said, "Kari, I'll bet you $50 you can't walk out of the door in the subacute therapy room. It's about 20 feet, and I don't think you can make it."

Gin gave me a sharp stare that could only mean, "Lu, why are you demotivating Kari by asking her to do something she just can't do yet!"

But Kari responded enthusiastically, taking me up on my bet. And before I knew it she had not only walked out the door, but had gone all the way down the hall.

Kari and I both grinned at Gin in triumph!

* * * * *

As the weeks continued to pass, we headed down a new stretch of the road back —an opportunity we'd hardly dared to dream about a few months before. With Kari progressing so well, the therapists hinted that soon we might be able to take her out in the car for some excursions. "Maybe," she said, "she could even spend an afternoon at home."

Excitement rippled through the three of us—Ginger and Kristin and me. We could hardly believe our ears! Was it possible that soon our family life would be like old times, with the four of us living together again under the same roof? Though the therapists were only talking about one afternoon excursion, it was a clear and wonderful signal to us: Before long, Kari would be coming home, eventually to stay. After those excruciating months with Kari in a coma, living with the uncertainty of her outcome, we were finally going to see her back where she belonged.

Kari's first trip home was made in the Daniel Freeman van. Two of the therapists loaded Kari into the vehicle and rode with her. They wanted to be there during this first time out, to make certain we could handle Kari at home. As her parents who had taken care of her all her life, it was a peculiar feeling to know they would be watching how we handled her, and they had the authority to decide whether or not we could continue to take her home. They needed to do a home evaluation, informing us as to what ramps and handrails we would need to install so Kari could navigate the wheelchair in the house. They also helped us identify other items that were necessary to convert the downstairs bedroom and bathroom so they would be handicapped-accessible for Kari.

We awoke that morning feeling so excited. This was the first day in months that Kari would be home; it felt like years. We couldn't wait to see her reactions. We thought she would be deliriously excited. We certainly were. We had high hopes the familiar surroundings of our home would help make some magic connection in Kari's brain and that her recovery would then speed along.

But when she was wheeled in she seemed so quiet. The smile we had so eagerly anticipated was not there.

We wheeled her around, showing her everything on the first floor. No real response. We wheeled her onto the patio and hoped the pool might be the connecting spark. Nope! Maybe her beloved cats, Max or Larkin....She seemed to recognize them but still was quiet and reticent. This was certainly not the enthusiastic response we had envisioned. We tried to ignore our disappointment.

The therapy team spent much of the time teaching us how to get Kari's wheelchair up and down the steps around our house and making lists of all the adaptive equipment they felt we would need when Kari came home again. So the first visit ended up being pretty mechanical. Fortunately, we passed muster and it got us ready for the second visit, which turned out to be quite an adventure.

The day began when we picked up Kari midmorning and took her out of the hospital by ourselves, with no nurses around to help. Getting Kari into the car was our first challenge. Kari at that time had casts on her leg and her arm, which made figuring out the angles for the transfer difficult. We finally found the right trajectory and stuffed her into the front seat. We were all so excited. Nothing was going to stop us!

Kari, Gin, and I settled into the car ourselves, with a sigh of relief, and at last I turned the key and started the engine. Kari nonchalantly leaned forward and changed the radio station. She had been notorious for changing radio stations as long as we could remember, always searching for that perfect song, and never wanting to listen to a single commercial.

This habit of Kari's had once been a source of irritation to me. Now it was a minor miracle. For some reason, Kari II was acting just like Kari I.

* * * * *

On this trip we gained some insight into Kari's less-than-excited response to her first visit. She seemed totally confused as we approached our home and drove into the Palos Verdes neighborhood where we lived.

We kept prodding her, asking questions about the neighborhood.

"Kari, there's Peninsula High, your old high school. See it? It's there on the right."

"Kari, look! There's the grocery store. Remember? We always shop there."

We had expected her to respond with the same excitement we felt. But Kari was silent for quite a while. Again, she certainly wasn't responding as we'd expected her to. She was quiet and a bit dazed. Then she stunned us, because with single words and gestures and a lot of guessing on our part she managed to explain what was wrong. When we'd told her we were taking her home she'd thought it was the home *she* remembered—the one in northern California we had moved from six years before. Earlier in her life, we had lived in northern California, and she had spent some happy growing-up years there. Now, Kari had no memory of the last six years of her life in southern California. The brain repair had stopped short of current memories.

She went on to explain, as best she could, that our Palos Verdes neighborhood felt foreign to her. It wasn't at all what she had expected to see.

Despite this apparent gap in her memory, once we arrived at the house, Kari rolled into the living room, and then into the family room using her one good foot to propel her wheelchair along, again in search of something familiar. Then, in the kitchen, she found it—the telephone. Before I could say anything, she had wheeled herself across the tile floor, flipped open her address book, and picked up the handset. The three of us watched in amazement as she dialed a number.

"Hi, hi, hi?" she began.

Adrian had been Kari I's boyfriend. Before the accident I had not gotten to know him very well. I viewed him as just another one of Kari's tight group of friends. Afterward, however, his warmth and caring really played an important role in Kari's recovery, serving as a significant motivator for Kari at several critical steps.

Whatever Adrian asked of Kari, she strived to achieve. He was worried about her weight, which was now below 100 pounds, so he helped her write a promise down in her notebook that she would eat all her food. That helped us all by being able to remind her she had promised Adrian she would eat more. She would grin, sigh, and dig back into the dreaded hospital food.

So Kari had dialed Adrian's number and had begun a "conversation" with him. Unfortunately, all she seemed to be saying on her end was "yeah…yeah…yeah…yeah." It was incredibly difficult for her to speak, and it was perhaps an even greater effort for her to be understood. Still, as with everything else, Kari was willing to persevere. Somehow, through nothing more than repetition and inflection, she carried on the rather limited conversation with Adrian and managed to make plans for him to come over to the house to see her.

Part of me ached for her, knowing how fluent she longed to be. But the greater part of me was incredibly proud. How had she managed to make herself completely understood? Where had she found the courage to try in the first place?

As she struggled to replace the handset I tried to help, but she dismissed my assistance with a firm "No!" She carefully hung up the phone all by herself.

We realized that although Kari might have big gaps in her memory, she was obviously able to access parts of her memory in those gaps. As years have passed, we have continued to notice her memory catching up with time. She now even remembers some of her senior year, the year of the accident, the year before the birth of Kari II.

✳ ✳ ✳ ✳ ✳

In her last weeks at Daniel Freeman, Kari's day began at 8:00 A.M. with a wake-up nudge from a nurse. A therapist supervised her breakfast, with Kari working hard to feed herself. Danish rolls were easy to master as was drinking from a straw. Use of a fork for the scrambled eggs was coming along, but she still needed some assistance. After breakfast, it was time for personal care. Kari was learning to do a lot of the work herself, pulling on her t-shirts, washing her face, brushing her teeth, and combing her hair. As every parent knows, watching your child struggle while sitting there and doing nothing to help is not always the easiest thing to do. When your child is injured it is even harder. Of course everyone's objective was Kari's self-sufficiency, so our parental role transitioned from hands-on assistance to cheerleading.

At 9:30, it was time for therapy to begin in earnest. Kari was transferred into her wheelchair (She was still unable to move reliably by herself.) and rolled into the common area outside her room. After an hour of stretching and walking with the aid of her walker and the help of her therapist, she turned her attention to speech. At 11:00 she had group activities. At noon it was lunchtime and more work on the elusive art of getting more food into her mouth than onto the t-shirt and floor. Occupational therapists, dealing with hands and arms, took over after lunch. Then came more speech and physical therapy sessions.

By 3:30, Kari was done with her daily workout. By now she was more than happy to climb into bed to get rested up for her visitors.

Gin and I were so fortunate Kari had such loyal friends. They made sure one or more of them showed up at the hospital around dinnertime. This was a daily event Kari looked forward to throughout her hard work, and it gave us the opportunity to head home, knowing she was in loving company. Once her friends left, Kari watched a movie or two and fell asleep.

This gift of a few hours each evening allowed Gin and me to have time for one another and for Kristin. We struggled with guilt for not being there for Kristin more often, but through it all she matured so much.

Before long, Kari received a big payoff for all her hard work: plastic braces replaced her leg and thigh casts. The left leg was becoming strong and was functioning as her primary standing leg. The right was coming along, but more slowly and with some hypersensitivity on the bottom of her foot. Nonetheless, in spite of these inconveniences, Kari was now walking daily with her walker.

Gradually, the daily application of arm splints was reduced. Her arms became loose enough to reach up over her head, then to bend at the elbow to touch the top of her head, then to lower to the wheel rims of her wheelchair. Strength for long wheelchair pushes would come later. Figuring out how to open her seatbelt without assistance was still a big production. And by opening her hands adequately, she was able to grip a pole, a Styrofoam cup, and a burrito. Kari was making amazing progress.

One day Kari and I had a conversation about gaining weight. Kari pointed to her hips and said, "Gain weight, gain weight, gain weight." For some reason, she frequently said things in threes. Junk food helped her eat more and gain weight more rapidly, so a typical dinner now might consist of a full In-and-Out burger or multiple tacos from the Border. Kari liked a lot of protein and a little fruit, but not too many vegetables or salads. To supplement her eating, she drank five Ensure shakes a day along with what seemed to us like gallons of apple juice. The result was, after dropping to well below 100 pounds, that Kari was now up to 107 pounds.

"Looking good!" I told her one evening.

She smiled. And she winked.

Before long, the winks weren't as necessary as they had once been. Kari's speech improved significantly, her vocabulary increasing from a very few words to a few dozen, which she was beginning to offer without prompting. At this point the sentences were still composed of a single word, much as a child begins to speak, and usually repeated three times. Sometimes she would have to repeat the same thing time after time after time, even fifteen or twenty times. But she patiently kept repeating until we figured out what she was trying to say.

Kari's patience amazed us. But remembering the verbal person she intrinsically is, it made perfect sense she would do what she had to in order to communicate. *She loves people too much to give this up*, I thought. Kari and her speech therapist worked diligently on enunciation, synonyms, and sentence completion.

Now that she had gained strength, Kari realized she could venture out in her wheelchair under her own power. Never content to do just a little, Kari made her way from her bed to the outer doors, a distance of about 50 feet. She was soon able to set and release the brake and remove her leg rests without help. And after mastering radio changing in the car, Kari also successfully tackled her bed controls, which raised and lowered the head and foot of the bed, and controlled the TV and the stereo. By now, the signs were unmistakable. Kari was taking charge of her own life.

* * * * *

I had been out of work since November 1992, when I'd left Evernet. Before Kari's accident, four companies had expressed interested in recruiting me, but it was clear that any kind of steady employment during Kari's recovery was out of the question. I needed to be where she was. And I was lucky enough to be able to do this. So I took only very short-term consulting assignments, with brief hours and flexible commitments. However, since we weren't blessed with infinite financial resources, I started thinking about finding a new job near the end of summer 1993.

In the meantime, Gin and I were approaching our twenty-fifth wedding anniversary, which we would celebrate on August 24. Prior to the accident, we had discussed going on a springtime cruise in the Greek Isles or a *Windsong* cruise in the South Pacific. We had very much looked forward to celebrating in a spectacular way our twenty-five years together.

Since the accident we had spent only one night away from home or hospital, and even that had been in the company of friends. While Gin and I had spent countless hours together, we'd had no time whatsoever to focus on each other. Our hearts, minds, and souls were tangled up with our daughters' circumstances. Every ounce of energy we had was devoted to Kari's recovery and Kristin's nurturing. Now, with Kari doing so well, we made the decision to get away for a few days.

"How about Santa Fe?" Gin suggested one day as we discussed our anniversary. "It's not too far away, and it's a great place to relax."

"Sounds good to me," I said. I made the reservations that same night.

But wouldn't you know it? Just before we were scheduled to leave, another crisis arose. Kari was diagnosed as having something called reflex dystrophy syndrome, or the Civil War disease.

"What on earth does a Civil War disease have to do with Kari?" I asked the doctor, feeling perplexed and frustrated.

"During the Civil War," he explained, "many amputations took place on the battlefield, and the soldiers who lost limbs often experienced phantom pain where the limb had been. Kari is experiencing something similar in her right leg, even though it's still there."

"I don't understand. What's causing the phantom pain?"

"That's the point. Nothing is wrong. It's just a nerve reaction. We're using nerve blocks to try and alleviate the problem, but in the meantime, she's experiencing some discomfort."

Discomfort was hardly the word for the incredible pain Kari was feeling in her right leg. She wanted immediate relief, but her primary specialist was in Europe and we had to enlist a back-up colleague. We faced a difficult choice: Could we leave her in pain and take a break? She was in no danger, but we still debated about whether to make the trip or postpone it.

We recruited Gin's parents and decided to go.

Gin and I walked the colorful streets and shops of Santa Fe, enjoyed several great meals, and drove up to Taos. The trip was a pleasure, a blessed relief from the relentless pressure. But Gin and I never really got around to fully relaxing. Our thoughts, our feelings were at Daniel Freeman, not in New Mexico. Our souls were with Kari. It would be months before Gin and I returned to being a normal couple, to sharing life as husband and wife. We had changed our environment, but we couldn't change our obsession with our daughter.

Then, on Saturday, we telephoned the hospital. We were connected with Kari's room only to learn she was still in significant pain from the phantom problem in her right leg and foot. We could hear her sobbing desperately in the background. Our hearts were nearly ripped out.

Also complicating our getaway weekend was a tempting job opportunity for me with a company in Denver. On Thursday of our four-day trip, I flew to Denver for an interview, which went well, but ended with the unexpected announcement that the offer was contingent on a forthcoming acquisition. The corporation wanted me to remain on hold until they sorted things out. I was let down and a little sorry I'd interrupted our celebration. It felt like a waste of time.

But at the Denver airport, while waiting for the plane to return to Santa Fe, I glanced outside and caught my breath. A spectacular rainbow was shimmering across the sky. For me, rainbows have always been a prelude to good news. So despite the uncertainties about the Denver job, I was full of excitement when I returned to Santa Fe.

Sure enough, the next day, there were two phone calls. One was from the company in Denver informing me that the acquisition had fallen through. The other was from a business acquaintance of mine, wanting to talk with me about joining his new board and helping him raise the initial seed capital for a venture that planned to advertise residential homes for sale on public kiosks in San Diego. This was an ideal solution, allowing me to get heavily involved in a new business while maintaining a lot of time flexibility.

By deciding to stay close to Kari and waiting for the right time and the right place, I had become involved with the company that was the predecessor to the enormously successful Homestore.com. The rainbow's promise was more than fulfilled. The deal provided our family with financial security for the rest of our lives.

* * * * *

Three things contribute most to recovery from a brain injury: intelligence, friend-and-family support, and being under the age of twenty-one. Kari was blessed with all three, especially the strong support of her friends. In her days at Daniel Freeman, Kari's friends were incredibly faithful. They stopped by almost daily from the end of the school year and into the summer. Sometimes two or more kids even climbed into her hospital bed for a cuddle—another way for her to reestablish human contact.

At first, the weekend visits home seemed to be paving the way for Kari's return to society. Kari's friends gathered in the living room to listen to music and talk. She loved seeing people, listening to music, getting a hug or two, and hearing the week's stories. The friends helped fill in her memory gaps. Every day she was in the hospital, friends took total responsibility for being with Kari through the evening hours. And although Kari could not and did not originate conversation, she invariably responded to everyone's comments with great enthusiasm.

But once Kari began to go home more regularly, things changed. Kari's friends had been friends with Kari I. When Kari II came out of the hospital, they were excited and they were comfortable with her at one level, but most of the banter subtly moved away from her. She simply could not engage in expressive, emotive conversations. She struggled with finding the word to respond to something said, but before she could find it and say it out loud, the conversation had moved well beyond the point she was trying to address. Also, although her memory was starting to recover, many of her friend's stories still did not resonate.

For Kari, her friends' presence was human interaction, and she thrived on it. For her friends, it was fun for the moment, but it didn't hold their attention. Kari I was not there. They didn't really understand or relate to Kari II. Instead, they expected the old Kari to emerge. She did not. In August and September, as each person went off to college, the visits dwindled and almost stopped. Only Adrian stuck around.

✳ ✳ ✳ ✳ ✳

"I…want, want, want, go, go, go…mall!"

Kari told Gin her intentions one morning, a few short weeks before going home. And she went on to communicate that to go to the mall, a few things would have to be done. She needed clothes. She needed makeup. She needed a haircut. She was still struggling to speak clearly, but her message was unmistakable—Kari wasn't going to reenter her world again without the proper preparation.

There was a new sense of excitement around her room as we prepared for Kari's mall excursion. And once the weekend rolled around, we got serious. Saturday morning, we made special arrangements for Rick, our hairdresser, to style her hair. At Harbor-UCLA, Gin had cut off one matted portion, and the surgeons had shaved off another, so Kari had ended up with long hair on only one side and in the back. Gin had done some rough shaping at the hospital, but up until now, Kari's coiffure had not received any professional attention.

By the time Rick was finished, Kari II looked wonderful. With short hair, a very lean body, and eyes that appeared bigger than life, Kari was a beauty again—not just to us, but to everyone who saw her. I couldn't help but notice young men were beginning to check her out. And Kari was remembering—with surprising success—how to flirt.

From Rick's, we took her to the mall. Kari had a cast on her left leg, so it stuck straight out. She also had a cast on one arm. Cruising between racks of clothes was a real challenge. More than once, she inadvertently dragged a couple of items off a rack as we pushed her through a store.

Wheeling Kari through Benneton, I was constantly talking to her, trying to jog her thoughts. Kari was quite a sight with her casts. But you would never have guessed she was newly home from a serious hospitalization. Most people probably thought she had simply broken a couple of limbs.

I was so proud of Kari's progress. I wanted to shout to the world, "Look at my daughter! See how well she's doing?" I felt excited, proud, exhilarated, accomplished. Making our way through the mall that wonderful Saturday, I realized I was feeling the way I had expected to in June, when I'd imagined wheeling her across the stage at her graduation.

Since then another season had come and gone, time had done its healing work, and this was better than I'd dared hope. It was more than a father's fantasy. It was more than an optimist's obsession. That Saturday, the dream really did come true.

Kari was back.

CHAPTER EIGHT

Live and Learn

On the bulletin board in Kari's hospital room hung a large-print calendar where Gin, Kristin, and I marked her past milestones and future appointments. It not only helped Kari get to physical therapy on time, but it also provided a visual reminder of how well she was doing. We made a point of highlighting bigger and better accomplishments along Kari's road to recovery.

One morning in late August, a couple of Kari's doctors came into her room. As we talked, Dr. Ludwig suddenly asked, "What would you say if we let Kari go home in a few weeks?"

"You mean home for good?" I smiled. "Why don't we ask her?"

Kari's face broke into a hopeful grin.

"Yeah, yeah, yeah!" Kari responded, beaming with delight.

"Her weekend releases have been consistently successful," he continued, "so it looks like this might be a good time to get ready for her transition home."

"What date were you thinking of?"

"It's only approximate, you know, three to four weeks."

"Like around…"

He glanced at the calendar, and thought for a minute. "Say around September 21. Of course," he added cautiously, glancing at his colleague, "this is all dependent on whether she continues to improve."

"We'll be ready," I assured him. "No problem with that."

Gin walked over and marked the date on the calendar where Kari could see it—the most important date we'd ever posted there. And although in the doctors' eyes September 21 was only an approximation, once it was marked in ink on the calendar, Kari locked on it with all her might. She labeled every day as "release minus eighteen days" or "release minus fifteen days." That date became the focus of her life. Like a little child counting the hours until Christmas morning, Kari's enthusiasm was boundless.

At "release minus ten days," however, some of Kari's therapists began to question the time line.

"We're thinking she might benefit from staying a few weeks longer," an occupational therapist confided out of earshot from Kari, a worried look on her face. "Maybe until early October."

"What about Kari's morale?" I retorted. "Can't you see how excited she is? She's counting the days."

"I know. That makes it difficult," she agreed. "But she could really use some more work on her arms and fingers."

"Since Labor Day," Gin explained, "all her friends have started leaving. They've gone away to college."

"That's right. And it's not the same for her now." I added. "Her evenings here are lonely and boring. She needs to be at home."

"I think being at home with her family will give her a new lease on life," noted Ginger, "after five and a half months of hospital schedules and food. Enough is enough."

"I couldn't agree more," I concurred. "To keep her here past the target date would devastate her."

"But what about her exercises?" the other therapist argued. "You want her to get full use of her hands and legs, don't you?"

I thought for a moment. "We've learned how to help her with other things. Why can't we learn how to help her do her exercises at home?"

The therapists paused, thinking over the possibilities. "You'll have to keep a log and we'll need to check it when we see her."

"No problem!" I said. "If that's all it takes, we've got a deal. Besides, she'll be coming back here for outpatient services anyway. She'll be in better shape than ever."

On September 21, after 148 days in Daniel Freeman, Gin and I hosted a "Get out of Jail" breakfast party for the therapists, nurses, doctors, and staff who had played such an indispensable part in Kari's recovery. It was an emotional time, a day of rejoicing, not only for us but for the entire the staff. Everyone had done a magnificent job. That breakfast was a happy celebration for all concerned.

Gin and I both felt moved and grateful as we said our goodbyes. We felt connected with almost every person there. But as we rolled Kari out of Daniel Freeman and toward our waiting car, she kept repeating, "Out of here. Out of here. Out of here. Right now. Right now. Right now."

✳ ✳ ✳ ✳ ✳

Because Kari needed help at night getting out of bed to go to the bathroom, Gin decided to sleep in Kari's room for a few weeks. And it was more than a matter of convenience—it was a huge support to Kari during that critical time of transition and readjustment.

One of the last remaining physical problems before bringing Kari home was getting her feet to lie flat against the floor. Therapy wasn't an option. The doctors scheduled another date for surgery, during which they both lengthened her leg tendons again and inserted pins into her toes to keep them straight. We weren't as frightened about the anesthesia this time. After the foot surgery, Kari recovered reasonably quickly. She immediately went to work on mastering the art of getting out of her wheelchair, rising to a standing position, and smiling in triumph when she succeeded.

She never ceased to amaze me. Whatever she lacked in physical capability, Kari always made up for in enthusiasm.

Even after this surgery Kari couldn't get out of bed by herself at first. Gin's help during the night was crucial for those middle-of-the-night bathroom visits since Kari was once again back in the wheelchair.

Every night Gin told Kari story after story as they lay in bed together. And Kari couldn't get enough of Gin's storytelling. Emotionally, at that point, Kari was like a five-year-old—she wanted nothing more than motherly comfort and a bedtime story before falling asleep. And of course she loved what she heard, because all of Gin's stories had a single theme: Kari, the princess, was finding her prince and living happily ever after.

From the moment she had awakened from the coma, Kari had demonstrated an intense interest in boys. If a decent-looking male came into the room, she would invariably smile in a flirtatious way and try to get his attention. Nonetheless, we could sense her insecurity. She felt unsure, in her condition, about whether she could actually attract and keep a boyfriend. Gin reassured her again and again, through the stories, that she really would find the love of her life. Like Gin, I was quite sure that some day Kari's prince really would come along.

In the meantime, there was more to Gin's all-night vigil than telling stories. When Kari woke up in the middle of the night, Gin had to wake up, too, from a sound sleep. She got up, transferred Kari to the wheelchair, helped her onto the toilet, and lifted her back into the wheelchair and then back into the bed. Sometimes this happened several times a night. During those weeks, Gin endured around-the-clock physical work, lifting and bending, and she handled it with incredible patience and endurance. But to this day Ginger's injured back continues to pay the price.

Gin had the patience and courage I lacked in dealing with Kari's hand and finger exercises. A few weeks after moving home, Kari was admitted to Long Beach Memorial for yet another surgery, this time on her elbow to remove a deposit of calcium that had formed, which limited her ability to bend her arm. While under general anesthesia the surgeons not only straightened out her arm, but also cast her fingers into a neutral position.

The casts were removed before we took her home. Our agreement with the staff when they released her was to do finger stretching exercises at home. We were told that if we did not keep up these exercises we would lose all the range we had gained during the surgery. I am normally quite capable of imposing necessary discipline, but I couldn't cope with the excruciating pain Kari faced every time she did those finger exercises.

Gin likened the nightmarish exercises to pushing your finger back as far as you can, and then having it pushed back another whole inch. I tried several times to take charge, to edge her forward, to encourage her to push herself to the max, but I just couldn't cope with her suffering. My heart broke when she cried out in pain, and again and again I found myself recoiling from the situation. This infuriated Gin and Kristin, who thought I was refusing to do my part. They hated doing this as much as I did and usually ended up crying as hard as Kari. On more than one occasion, we had shouting matches, then wept bitterly afterward.

We had been told that if Kari didn't do the exercises properly, there would have to be more surgeries. The worst-case scenario was that her hands would be permanently crippled. I knew all that. I understood it very well. I just couldn't face the agony of those sessions. After many a verbal explosion, Gin and I finally settled the matter by reversing our usual roles. She became the physical therapist, pushing Kari to new lengths. I became the comforter and nurturer after each session.

In hindsight we would never put anyone through pain like this. Eventually, Kari did have to have more surgery to get back the use of her right hand. All that torture (and believe me when I say it was torture for all four of us) was for naught! I felt vindicated, but it was a hollow victory.

* * * * *

The other side of the early days after release from Daniel Freeman was the indomitable spirit Kari possessed and expressed.

About three months into Kari's recovery, we began to publish a newsletter called *The Road Back*. The newsletter was our way of keeping a group of friends who were invested in Kari's recovery informed without having to spend endless hours on the phone rehashing the same stories. At its peak we were sending out more than three hundred copies of the newsletter and I'm told that through duplication the circulation reached over a thousand.

Our newsletter captured Kari's spirit in an interview we published in March of 1994.

> *Kari continues to improve significantly month by month. In order to capture a little of her spirit, she agreed to an interview with The Road Back. When interviewed, Kari was lounging on her waterbed distracted by a mom,*

a cat, and papers she wanted to look at on her bed. In other words, it was a typical Sunday afternoon.

The Road Back: In April it's been a year since the accident. How do you feel about the year?

Kari: It's hard to say. There are so many emotions. I've met so many wonderful friends at therapy.

The Road Back: What do you remember about the accident?

Kari: Nothing! I want to wake up. 1…2…3…nothing happened?

The Road Back: What are some of your first memories after you woke up from the accident?

Kari: Courtney's hair cut. My friends saying, "Kari, what's your name?" Dumb!

The Road Back: What are you looking forward to the most?

Kari: Going to college, getting married, and having a family.

The Road Back: How have you viewed your friends this past year?

Kari: I hate them (long donkey laugh)! Not! My friends have meant a lot this year. Thank you for standing by me.

The Road Back: Could you have made it through this last year without them?

Kari: No. Never. I would have died.

The Road Back: What have been the best things about therapy?

Kari: Friends at therapy—especially Lynn.

The Road Back: What have been some special days?

Kari: Misto's (restaurant), Universal Studios, and trips to Santa Barbara and San Diego.

The Road Back: How have you improved in the last month?

Kari: Walking a lot better. My hands have opened up. My right hand is much better.

The Road Back: What music do you like?

Kari: Rock n Roll. Not! Love songs.

The Road Back: What things strike you as funny?

Kari: Adrian's mom reading my sexy love letters to him on the phone. The last line of the movie *Greedy.* My hee-haw laugh. Listening to friends tell me stories.

The Road Back: What do you want for your birthday?

Kari: To walk, to speak better, and a little kitten. (Dad says no way!)

The Road Back: What do you want to tell your friends?

Kari: I love getting letters from friends even if they say, "Hi. Bye. I love you."

The Road Back: What do you say when people say you look good?

Kari: Don't hate me because I'm beautiful! (Laughs and laughs)

* * * * *

For me, the most fascinating and rewarding experience of all was watching Kari's mind repair itself. I consider myself something of a technologist, so I'm fairly well versed about how computers operate. Kari's mind worked like a database that had become corrupted. Once it realized the problem, it went to work reconnecting and rebuilding.

Our human minds normally have what a computer geek would term "high bandwidth." Normally, we are able to do many tasks simultaneously. For instance, when we drive, we have to watch all around for other cars. While we are doing this, we remain conscious of our speed. We may, in the meantime, be listening to the radio and talking to someone. We are also thinking about where we are going and making the appropriate turns.

One typical minute of our conscious life is filled with layers of mental multiprocessing.

As Kari came out of the coma she had a seriously one-track mind. She literally could not "walk and chew gum at the same time." When we sat down to dinner with her, for example, we had to remember that she could only eat—she was unable to talk and listen *and* eat. If she tried, she lost control. That would change, but it would happen slowly.

The human brain also seems to have a storage place where it indexes the things we learn. If I were to ask you what new thing you learned today, you could retrieve that information from a specific location in your brain. You'd access it, remember it, and tell me about it. But there was no buffer to tell Kari II what was new information and what was old. When Kari remembered something, the brain's new reconnection bypassed the storage place to tell her she now remembered something that she could not access the day before.

She had to learn how to remember.

Still, in spite of all her limitations, Kari was excited about life and thrilled with every conquest she made. More and more, she wanted to reconnect with people. Maybe that's why, at Freeman one day during outpatient treatment, she got the bright idea that she'd like to go hang out with some friends down the street. And that's exactly what she did.

As usual, that morning we had dropped Kari off for therapy on the ground floor of the main Freeman building. Throughout the day, Kari had 45-minute therapy sessions: occupational, physical, speech, recreational, and group. Because these sessions could not always be scheduled back to back, Kari often had to wait in the outpatient lobby in the basement. The receptionist there developed a special relationship with Kari, often chatting with her. This appealed to Kari far more than the hours of passive TV watching she had to do when she was left alone.

That particular day, probably because the receptionist was busy and distracted, Kari somehow decided she'd rather talk to somebody than sit still. Maybe she'd just go over to an adjacent building and drop in on one of her friends. Her hands and arms were not yet strong enough to push the wheelchair, but by using her one good foot for propulsion, Kari moved herself along. She traveled along the hall, up the elevator, out the door. And somehow, despite the fact that it bordered a busy street, she managed to make her way down the outside sidewalk and safely into the other building.

When the therapist came out to get Kari for her next session, she was gone. Both therapist and receptionist immediately panicked. They urgently called security. Security, in turn, broadcast a page over the Freeman intercom. It took them a half hour to find Kari. It would have taken longer, but fortunately an aide at the other building called the main desk. "There's a young woman in our waiting room," she explained, "trying to talk to people. I'm not sure who she is, but she's in a wheelchair…"

We knew nothing about this little episode until we arrived at the hospital to pick her up.

Kari smiled gleefully as the tale was told. She was as proud as she could be about her daring adventure. Despite the dangers, we were elated hearing about her initiative and creativity. This was vintage Kari I. In days gone by, if she'd wanted to see someone, rather than ask permission, she'd just go. Nowadays, although we were concerned about her safety, we couldn't help but see this latest incident as a positive event. On the way home we offered the appropriate safety instructions. "You have to be careful, Kari," we repeated more than once. But try as we might, we couldn't hide our smiles.

* * * * *

Helping Kari return to the real world had long been my goal, and her unscheduled wheelchair excursion convinced me she was ready for more activity than Daniel Freeman's outpatient programs could possibly offer. Even before her final release from the hospital, during one of her weekends at home, we had taken Kari to Universal City. One of the highlights of that particular theme park is the Back to the Future Ride, which creates the illusion of traveling back in time, much like the movie of the same name. The visual illusion is accomplished through dramatic special effects, which involve lights and rapidly moving images.

In my enthusiasm to reengage Kari with life, however, I had forgotten about the warning that brain-injured patients sometimes have seizures, which can be triggered by strobe lights or other intense sensory bombardment. As I was completing Kari's transfer from her wheelchair into the Back to the Future ride, with everyone waiting on us so the ride could get started, it suddenly dawned on me that the ride's visual stimulation might well trigger a seizure.

My heart sank. But in the same instant, I also knew it was too late to turn back.

Kari was already buckled in, and her wheelchair was being pulled back from the tracks. We were committed. As we settled into the ride, I paid careful attention to Kari and made sure my arm was around her so she knew she was going to be okay. I watched her face intently and constantly, searching for signs of distress. Fortunately, there were no problems, but the ride left me feeling shaken. I was well aware I had done something both risky and imprudent.

The rest of the day, we chose easygoing rides like the tram, from which we watched a short "movie" being filmed. No more excitement for us! Instead, I leisurely pushed Kari around the park in her wheelchair, talking to her, leaning slightly forward as she rolled along. It was sheer delight just to be with her outdoors, in a theme park, riding rides, seeing her smile at people and say hello to them, interacting with others and experiencing life. Kari was reemerging in a way that, six months before, I could not have imagined.

With that first successful theme park experience in mind, now that Kari was home to stay, I got the idea it was time for another one. While Gin was off with her tennis group one weekend, I took Kari to Knott's Berry Farm by myself—our first father-daughter outing since the accident.

The best ride at Knott's Berry has always been the whitewater rapids, where a round "boat" comes hurtling down a water chute, and everybody gets soaked. Like everyone else in our family, Kari has always loved theme parks, so even though it was February and a bit chilly, I decided to go for it.

The Knott's staff helped me get Kari into the boat. And once we buckled her seatbelt, away she and I went, bobbing and spinning as gallons of water streamed into the boat. We were quickly soaked, but laughed our heads off in the process. This was just the release Kari needed. And when the Knott's staff saw how much fun everyone had, they gave everyone in our boat another ride without requiring us to get back in line.

Some of the people who rode with us were tourists from Scotland, and one member of their party was also disabled. Naturally, we developed an instant camaraderie. They wanted to hear the whole story about Kari, and by the time we'd made two loops around the waterway, we were all great friends. Kari's infectious smile has never failed to engage those who meet her. And even back then, although her communication skills were far more limited than they are now, she somehow managed to keep her new friends' attention while she repeated herself until they understood what she was trying to say.

Because the outings to the parks worked so well, we began looking for other ways to phase Kari into society at large and to prepare her for self-sufficiency. In this regard, one group of wonderful people who came to play a huge role was the staff at Café Misto, where Gin and I had spent Kari's graduation evening.

A European-style family café, Misto's made room for Kari to navigate between the tables, even while she was still in her clunky wheelchair with her cast-bound leg sticking out at an odd angle. They interacted with her, embraced her, and cherished her. From servers to cooks to busboys to managers, everyone at Misto's applauded Kari's ongoing recovery. They made her feel both normal and special. Over the next three years following Kari's release from the hospital, we ate there from two to four times every week. As regular guests, it was like dining in our own home. Meanwhile, our patronage played a major role in Kari's emergence into normal life and Kristin's desire for a career as a restaurateur.

* * * * *

In early 1994, our family went to Utah to spend some time with Gin's parents and to go skiing. One morning Gin and I got up early to hit the slopes while Kari and Kristin slept in. When we returned, both girls were aglow with excitement.

"What's up?" I asked.

"You're not going to believe it," said Gin's Mom, who was smiling broadly, too.

"Try me."

"Well, you know how Kari uses her wheelchair as a walker?" Kristin began, pausing dramatically. "Right?"

"Right." I could tell Kristin was taking her time with the story to tease me, and my curiosity was getting the best of me. "Of course I know that. So what happened?"

"Okay, okay. So here's what happened: When I got Kari out of bed this morning," said Kristin, "I let her get behind the wheelchair like she always does. But once she was up and ready, I sort of…pushed the chair away from her. Just a little bit"

"You did *what?*"

"I pushed the chair away from Kari. And she walked, Dad! She walked on her own!"

"Step after step. No assistance!" Gin's mom confirmed. "I saw it."

Gin and I were stunned.

"Kari, can you take a few steps now?" I asked, hoping against hope that she wasn't too tired to try. "Will you show us how you walked?"

Kari smiled. She stood up, steadying herself with the wheelchair handles, and moved around behind it. Then she let go and gently pushed it away. She took a step. Then another. No hands! She looked like Bambi on ice, awkward, crooked, and unsteady. I was afraid I'd have to catch her in midair at any moment. But she was walking. Really walking. Walking all by herself.

I flashed back to twenty years before when, as a toddler, Kari had walked for the first time. That was expected. We were waiting, as all parents do, for baby's first steps. This was so very different. Kari II's first steps had never been a sure bet; we had no guarantee they would ever happen. This was a bonus, an unplanned blessing. I couldn't have felt more proud or more grateful.

Those first steps were especially good news, because Gin and I were beginning to think Kari had become wheelchair dependent, too comfortable and willing to settle for less than full mobility. I had been secretly devising ways to disrupt Kari's comfort zone so her wheelchair-bound days would be numbered. Thankfully, I didn't have to activate my plans. Kristin had done it for me.

From that day on, Kari increased the amount of time she walked day by day, week by week. I think this was the real beginning of Kari's independence. Now that she was moving around on her own, we knew she would eventually be able to fully function without our help. Maybe now Kristin could begin to get the affirmation and attention she so richly deserved.

Kristin had become our forgotten child. She was a sophomore in high school the year of Kari's accident. For months, Gin and I were gone, virtually living at the hospital. Of course Kristin needed as much consideration as Kari, and we did our best to give her some quality time. But because of the endless hospital schedule we kept, our involvement in Kristin's life was necessarily limited.

Kristin had a difficult time dealing with the accident. It was as if she had lost everyone—both her sister and parents were gone, and she was left on her own more than any of us would have wanted. When Kari came home from the hospital, Kristin was wonderful about being available for Kari. But she needed a life, too. She needed to be able to have fun with her friends without worrying about Kari or feeling guilty.

Fortunately for us, the pain that Kristin experienced didn't cause her to act out her frustrations in negative or destructive ways. How easily that could have happened, and she would have had good reason. But Kristin was self-contained and balanced. She helped us, she cared for her sister, and ultimately she served as the catalyst for Kari's first efforts to walk.

Now that Kari was walking, both she and Kristin were free.

* * * * *

Shortly after becoming ambulatory Kari approached her first two anniversaries. April 2 was the one-year anniversary of the "U-turn heard 'round the world." On April 5, Kari turned nineteen. A few days before that major date, while sitting on our blue leather sofa, I remarked to Kari, "It's been a spectacular year. In no other year in your life have you improved so much!" Kari laughed. I was finishing up a beer and absentmindedly began to blow into the bottle to make the foghorn sound. Kari took up the unintended challenge and asked for the bottle. She leaned her shoulder into me and gave me a teasing push while grabbing the bottle. I played the game knowing full well that she could not possibly do the lip formations required to make that low warning sound.

"Kari, I'll bet you a kitten that you can't make the foghorn sound!" Kari wanted a kitten for her birthday more than anything else. I had put my foot down because we already had two other cats. My Kari instinct, though, told me that here was an opportunity to join progress, achievement satisfaction, and the granting of a birthday wish.

There was no hesitation in response to this challenge. She laughed and looked for a long time at the bottle and then experimented with a lot of lip formations and slowly the sound began to emerge. At first I could deny that she had really accomplished the goal of the bet, but soon the sound was loud and clear. Kari started screaming with unrestrained joy, which caused us to laugh so hard we were crying. When my tears settled, I committed to buy any type of kitten she wanted.

A few days later Kari picked up a black and brown tabby Persian kitten we aptly named U-Turn or Youi for short. Even in my naming of the cat, I showed how we continued to embrace and incorporate the event that had stopped our lives and restarted them on a new more positive path.

* * * * *

While life might have been coming in before on little cat's feet, it was roaring in with tiger ferocity now. When Kari was first starting to come home from the hospital, she reestablished her love for music. The first thing she manipulated was the car radio to change from one station to another to find the music that she likes. The first artist she could identify by name was Bryan Adams. In early May, Kari heard on the radio that Bryan Adams was playing a concert in L.A. in June. She mentioned more than once that she really wanted to go.

I happened to have a friend, Kris Friedrich, who struck up a relationship with Rick Dees, a very successful local radio personality and the host of a popular weekly Top 40 national show. I called Kris to ask if it might be possible to get some tickets from KISS-FM for the concert. The request snowballed into a fabulous day for the Karster as Kris decided to push Rick to have her as an on-air guest. Additionally, Kris insisted he would provide his corporate limousine to pick up Kari and take her to the show. Kris had heard the story of Kari's disappointment that I didn't arrange for a limo in her past on the infamous birthday event at the Forum.

At 7:30 A.M., Kari was picked up with her sister Kristin and her dad in a long sleek, black limousine to go to the KISS studios to meet Rick Dees and receive the tickets on the air. Rick and Ellen Kay, his morning partner, came down the hall to greet us before our segment. While back-to-back songs were playing, we were briefed and outfitted with our headsets for the on-air interview. When Rick asked how many years difference there was between the two girls, Kari looked down at her hands and held out two fingers. She was in the process of mentally going "one, two" to get to the right answer when her sister took charge of the answer. Kari was a fabulous hit with her now patented donkey laugh and several repetitions of "right on, right on," which she had promised two of her friends to say on the air.

* * * * *

As the summer progressed, Gin and I talked more and more about the need for Kari to get away on a trip by herself. Not really by herself, but without either of us being there. It had now been almost a year and a half since the accident and we wanted to push the envelope. We asked Kari to pick one of her friends and to pick a destination. The friend was one of her twin friends, Mimi, and the destination was Club Med in Mexico. For a painful week, we second-guessed ourselves. Was Kari really ready to go out with only a peer friend? Was she responsible enough? Would she be too much of a support burden for Mimi?

As the plane landed and Kari disembarked full of rich stories, and telling them with less aphasia, we knew that we had taken a successful risk. Trip. Talk better. Trip. Walk better. Trip. More integrated into the mainstream of life. Trip. Cognitive gains.

* * * * *

By now, Kari was feeling the full effects of her old friends drifting away. Not many of us retain our high school friends but this breakup was especially impactful for Kari. We usually break the bonds of high school because we establish new relationships in college or the work world. Our interests change. Kari lost, but she was having trouble replacing.

In many ways, Kari was like a very young teenager seeking her independence. And that independence, in Kari's mind, had everything to do with dating. So after learning to walk again, Kari began to actively seek relationships with young men. Unfortunately, her limited ability to see the dangers of her actions was troubling to all of us.

Following her brain injury, Kari's judgment was significantly impaired. A brain injury forces the brain to simplify. When an uninjured person decides to act, she passes her impulse through a set of filters and the brain considers the implications of the act to see if it's appropriate. Kari was still incapable of this kind of multiprocessing. If she thought about an action, there were few, if any, filters applied. Kari I and Kari II had similar impulses. The difference was all in the filters—Kari I had had several; Kari II had virtually none.

We never had harsh words for Kari II. How could we? Instead, we tried to guide her, gently as possible, toward a better understanding of the risks she was taking. We sought to help her foresee the consequences that might result. Our objective was a full recovery. A cocoon was not going to get us there.

During the summer of 1994 we began to look for a female companion for Kari, someone to live with us on a full-time basis. We figured that a twenty-year-old needed to do things with someone her own age. Networking through friends, we made contact with a Swedish girl who wanted to live in the United States. We arranged for her to come to California in the fall to be Kari's driver and companion. But before she arrived, Kari met Matt. He was her classmate in an Acquired Brain Injury program in Santa Monica, which Kari began in the fall of 1994.

While drunk, Matthew had crashed his motorcycle on the Oakland Bay Bridge, and the resulting head injury had severely impacted his short-term memory. He could tell you any fact that could be retrieved from his long-term memory but could not remember what he'd had for dinner an hour earlier. Kari's repeated speech and slight limp let people know in a subtle way that something traumatic had happened in her life. Matthew was physically unscarred by his accident. Nonetheless, he was a damaged young man.

From the minute she laid eyes on him, Kari had been captivated. She'd started flirting and flattering and doing everything in her power to get him to respond. We knew all about Kari's infatuation. But one day, I received a call in my office from Ginger.

"Congratulations, you have a son."

"What? What do you mean by that?" I said, already smiling, knowing very well what Gin was about to tell me.

"I mean Matthew."

"Matthew? Kari's Matthew? That's super! But how did he become my son?"

"Long story. I'll give you the sordid details when you get home."

It seems that Matt had been living with a woman on the west side of L.A., who was supporting him while he recuperated. She'd been taking care of his needs, and let's just say that in his own way, he'd been taking care of hers. When this woman found out that Matt was interested in Kari, she had thrown all of his belongings out on the lawn and told him to find someplace else to live. End of relationship.

Of course, for Kari's sake, Gin and I adopted Matt. We invited him to move in with us. He was soon able to drive and quickly became an enormous help in Kari's transportation.

When Matthew first came into our lives, I thought he might be a great future husband for Kari. He was good-looking, intelligent, and seemed to find Kari very special. With Kari's expressive limitations, I was amazed she was able to "capture" him. And his companionship did great things for Kari. Being around him provoked enormous improvements in her walking, talking, and memory.

But within a year, Kari had started to outgrow Matthew. We felt he made his own limitations larger by refusing to accept, understand, or cope with them. Kari, on the other hand, refused to be limited by her accident. She wanted to grow, to improve, and to become a fully functional woman. To do so, even she could see she would have to leave Matthew behind. While Matthew was still living with us in the house, their relationship evolved from boyfriend-girlfriend to just companions. Matt's new responsibility was to take Kari places while watching out for her safety.

With Matthew in tow, Kari started going out more. Where does a twenty-something woman go to look for a guy? The students in Kari's brain injury classes were wonderful friends, but Kari wanted to make it in the mainstream for a serious relationship. So she tried the bar scene.

For the most part, Kari's subsequent dating encouraged Gin and me. We knew that she needed to meet lots of people and sort out for herself what she wanted in a relationship. Just as she'd rediscovered other aspects of her personality, Kari needed to get in touch with her sexuality.

During this period of time, Kari went out with several dozen young men. Most of the time we were smart enough to keep our views to ourselves, facing the classic parental paradox: How could we allow our daughter to have enough experiences to grow, without putting her in jeopardy? We tried to help her think clearly without giving her mandates that she would feel obligated to reject or rebel against.

One night when we were out of town and Kari was home for a brief time by herself, she decided to call a taxi and go to a bar in Redondo Beach. We learned later—to our horror—that the cab driver had aggressively come on to her and had become insistent about having sex with her. Somehow, some way, Kari had managed to get herself out of the cab and safely into the house.

It was another narrow escape, but Kari had made it through again.

Kari's post-accident dating life wasn't always the way we wanted it to be. It wasn't always pretty. It wasn't always easy. But Kari was learning. And we soon came to see that she was preparing herself for the "prince" Gin had told her about in all the bedtime stories.

* * * * *

Through the next couple of years, Kari continued to make enormous progress. From a distance in retrospect, she moved consistently and quickly. From up close as we lived it, we found moments of boundless joy followed by months of sameness. Through the months and quarters we stayed true to our metaphor. Kari I was dead and Kari II was improving. Kari II gave us moments to inspire us. Kari II gave us moments that scared us. To be true, we had to let Kari II grow and develop as we had Kari I. This time we compressed the years from birth to eighteen into three or four years. How many of us have said that if we had our parenting jobs to do over again, we would do it so much better? We got to do Kari over again but it was so different.

When Kari first went to Santa Monica in the fall of 1994 for their Acquired Brain Injury program, we were really stretching a point and were indulged by a wonderful director of the program. Stretching Kari provoked growth and gave her comfort that she could live in the mainstream world.

While much progress and joy happened from the spring of 1994 to the spring of 1997, so much more was about to happen to Kari II as she entered adulthood for the second time.

* * * * *

Throughout both of her lives, I had always had a sixth sense about Kari's readiness to do something new. After the accident, I could feel change coming long before it arrived. As Kari painfully and powerfully moved through her rehabilitation, the physical therapists had predicted she would most likely be able to walk, but that she would never be able to run again.

As with so many other negatives we'd encountered along the way, that prognosis really spurred us on. The previous Thanksgiving, Kari had astounded us by returning to snow skiing. With the help of outrigger poles and the incredibly supportive staff of the National Ability Center in Park City, Utah, Kari had been helped into her skis. When we saw her come down the bunny slope showing an obviously weak right side but also the unmistakable signs of a parallel skier, joy, elation, and pride expressed itself through the now familiar flow of a misting of tears. Skiing! What else was she going to be able to conquer?

In the midst of Kari's dating escapades, one spring day in 1997, my sister Lisha came to our home in Palos Verdes for a visit. We were all excited by the progress Kari had made. We sat around talking, and not surprisingly, Kari soon became the focal point of the conversation. I told Lisha all about Kari's first steps, and how she had been walking better and better ever since. Then, all of a sudden, an idea flashed through my mind.

"Kari," I announced. "I think you're ready to run."

Kari gave me that devastating smile of hers, and nodded vigorously. "Yes!" she answered. "Yes, yes!"

"Lu, are you sure?" Lisha looked a little worried.

Gin just shook her head.

"We'll see what happens," I shrugged. "But I have a gut feeling about this. Let's go out front."

All of us gathered in front of the house. I held out my hand. Kari took it. I started out at a very slow trot. At first Kari walked quickly, trying to keep up with me. But then I felt her put additional pressure on my hand and arm, and all at once she began to run. She was moving very unhurriedly, almost in slow motion. But there was no doubt about what she was doing.

"I'm running!" she exclaimed. "Running! Running!"

I was as ecstatic as Kari was. I suddenly remembered that terrible run I'd tried to take the morning after her accident. My legs had been almost as useless as hers that day. I had been immobilized, knowing she was precariously suspended between life and death.

Now, in what seemed like a lifetime later, Kari was actually running with me. My joy was so great my feet barely seemed to be touching the ground.

There wasn't much more I could ask for. Against all odds, Kari's miracles had followed one another in an astonishing procession. She had survived those first critical days. Her coma had ended. She had come home. She had learned to walk. She was speaking more clearly, more coherently, slowly but surely overcoming the aphasia that so restricted her communications skills. Kari was discovering new relationships. She was establishing boundaries for herself. She was learning to choose.

And now, Kari was running.

* * * * *

Shortly after Kari's run, the family was packing all our things and cleaning out the house. In February, I had persuaded Gin to go house hunting. Palos Verdes had been home to us for more than a decade. When we first bought the house there, I requested only one thing: I wanted a view. Of course, the house we eventually bought had everything but a view.

Now, there was a pressing need to consider a move. Palos Verdes did not have many young adults Kari's age. PV was home to couples and families, not singles. Gin was comfortable and well established. She had paid her dues in PV through volunteer work and had developed a broad friend network. However, ever the adventurer, she agreed to look at a specific location in Long Beach that would give the family a great combination of benefits: access to singles Kari's age on Second Street, a view of the water for me, and an easy commute to my office.

Gin and Kari looked for one day and found a house they fell in love with. I met Gin outside the house that evening to just take a look at its setting. There was a full moon low to the horizon framed by the palm trees and reflecting across the almost settled in for the night Alamitos Bay. From that point I didn't care what the house looked like, I was a buyer.

We moved in the summer of 1997 and began the search for the perfect man for Kari. She still held that unfulfilled dream in her heart, and we all shared it with her. As I looked at her, gorgeous and radiant and irrepressible, I couldn't help but believe her one true love was waiting somewhere, just around the corner.

After the move, Matthew and Kari would occasionally visit a coffee shop on the Alamitos Bay Peninsula. One of the shopkeepers was a California State Long Beach University graduate student, Dana Allen. Kari and Matt enjoyed talking with her and she moved from an acquaintance to a friend. When Matt announced that spring he was leaving, Kari proposed we invite Dana to live in the house. Dana could drive Kari to school and a woman companion would be far better to go trolling with.

We interviewed Dana and recognized her immediately as a younger Ginger. She was friendly, loving, caring, and responsible. She was instantly accepted by Kari as a close friend and by the family as a full member. She moved into our home in June 1997 as Matthew was leaving to live in an apartment down the Peninsula. Kari had moved a giant step closer to the mainstream world.

It's been a great year. However, I'm sure the best is yet to come.

CHAPTER NINE

"Today, Tomorrow and Forever..."

Kari had a romantic dream. Gin and I knew that, and in many ways we shared it. What we didn't know was that Kari was developing her own strategy for making her dream come true. With the help of her old beau, Matthew, who visited often, Kari had been surfing the Web. One night she had discovered she could post her picture, along with an ad, to let eligible bachelors know she was interested in meeting someone special. On love@aol.com, Kari uploaded her picture and responded to the server's questionnaire:

Relationship: Serious

Birth date: April 5, 1975

Love banner: Seeking long-term relationship

Country, state, city, zip code: USA, California, Long Beach, 90803

How far willing to travel: L.A./Orange County.

Mate target age range: 21–36

Your Height: 5' 7"

Mate's target height: 5' 6" to 6' 6"

Your body type: Slender

Preferred mate body type: Not important

Mate race: Not important
Mate religion: Not important
Mate marriage status: Single
Your money situation: Middle of line
Your drinking habits: Occasionally
Your smoking habits: Never
Music you like: Pop, country, R&B, blues, rap
You like to do: Going on walks, drawing, eating out, listening to music, dancing.
Add: I had a serious automobile accident making a U-turn not far from the house. I was in a coma for two and a half months and in the hospital for six months. I am still recovering now five years after the accident but I have made incredible progress and love life. I'm excited to be alive.

One night Ginger and I heard Matt and Kari busily typing as they sat at the computer down the hall.

"I wonder what's up," Gin said.

"Should we take a look?" I asked.

"I don't know," Gin hesitated.

Just then we heard Kari's voice. "Look at all this email!" she exclaimed. "What am I going to do with it?"

Gin and I strolled down the hall to Kari's desk area.

"Hi, Kar. Hi, Matt. What's up?" I said as casually as possible.

"Dad," Kari said. "Just look at all this email!"

"Where'd it come from?" I asked.

"From the Internet!" she said triumphantly. "Look at all the responses!"

"Responses?" I queried.

"Responses to my ad."

"Your ad?" asked Ginger, frowning slightly.

"Yeah, the ad I put on AOL, " Kari said. "You post your picture and then people write to you. Look how many letters I got!"

I looked at the screen and saw several hundred emails in her "in box."

Oh, my God.

"Too bad I can't read them very well," Kari said.

That's how we learned about her plan. Although I was very interested in helping Kari find higher caliber males than the ones she'd been meeting at the bars, I wasn't at all sure this way the way to do it.

A few days later, the family went to Ginger's parents' house in Park City for the Thanksgiving holiday. On Friday, after skiing for a couple of hours in the sparse early season snow, I wanted to spend some time with Kari.

"Kar-Kar, how about if we go through a bunch of your emails?" I said. Fortunately, I had a lot of time and I was interested to see what kind of romantic responses the Internet could bring. I read the emails to Kari and based on my understanding of what she wanted to say, typed a response to the sender. Kari added to it or changed things before pressing "send."

Like most parents, Gin and I had always heard how we should protect our children from the weirdos who lurk in the shadows of cyberspace. Ginger was worried about what kind of person would respond. For some reason, I wasn't. In fact, after reading the replies, I was honestly impressed with the quality of the men Kari heard from: people, who, like her, were looking for love on the Internet. A high percentage of the responses came from guys working in high-tech positions who were too busy to have a life. The Internet gave them a new window into the world.

Out of the first hundred, we found fifteen or so that deserved a response. Kari kept trying to look at their pictures, which she had done when Matt was helping her. But I wouldn't let her, insisting instead that she concentrate on inner attributes rather than outward appearance. In my responses on Kari's behalf, I indicated, "I have something called expressive aphasia resulting from my accident. It makes me sound far less intelligent than I am. It sounds like I have a serious stutter or have been drinking a bit too much." I wanted to lower the inquirers' expectations just a little so if someone phoned, he would be pleasantly surprised by Kari's abilities.

From those first fifteen replies, we found two that I thought were very special— from young men named Jason and Todd. Both showed a genuine emotional connection with Kari. I measured that connection not only in the words we read, but by the sensitivity that was laid between the lines.

The most significant response said,

Dear Kari,

Your posting at love@aol really touched me. From having been through such hardship with your accident, one would expect you to have a completely different attitude than what comes across on love@aol. Instead, the happiness, joy, and overall thankfulness for life shine through. I was recently diagnosed with Bell's palsy—a temporary infection of the facial nerve that causes slight paralysis of the face. I had been searching for someone to talk to about it without much success when I came across your posting. You've brightened my day and made me feel like no matter what happens with the Bell's palsy, I'll overcome. Have a wonderful day!

Todd

As soon as I read Todd's response, I knew he was a very special person. Kari's reply to him brought about an immediate exchange of phone numbers. And the moment Kari called him from Utah their courtship began.

Todd is an extraordinarily sensitive human being, and from the very start he was invariably patient with Kari as she slowly pronounced her words. Though Kari had made enormous progress in her expressive and emotive skills, she still had difficulty with extended conversations, and sometimes people became frustrated with her deliberate way of speaking. But there was never a moment of difficulty between her and Todd. His patience and understanding were saint-like. The two of them arranged to meet at our home and then to go to the Aquarium of the Pacific in Long Beach. After that first excursion, Todd was a regular visitor at our house.

Unlike so many other young men who had dated Kari, Todd was very comfortable being with her in family settings. The two of them went out to dinner with us, to Long Beach Pops concerts, or to hear music in the park. Intuitively understanding the important role Gin and I played in Kari's support system, Todd became a valued member of our family as well as a serious boyfriend.

We soon learned more about Todd's interesting childhood and his subsequent journey toward Kari. He had been raised by a single mom. After his parents' divorce, which had taken place while Todd was very young, he and his mother had moved to eastern Washington. There Todd had to learn the rural version of growing up, leaving behind his L.A. savvy. The challenges of this relocation dramatically increased Todd's capacity for empathy and kindness.

In his late twenties, Todd had come back to southern California to build his career, working long hours doing television promotions for NBC in Burbank. The Internet had provided him with a way to break out of his grueling routine.

And his chance discovery of Kari's ad allowed him to believe, perhaps for the first time in his life, that one special woman could be part of his world.

As Kari and Todd spent ever-increasing time together, Todd's family was as delighted with their relationship as we were. Connie, Todd's mom, fell in love with Kari right away, believing she was the answer to many prayers that her son would someday find Ms. Right. Even though I reminded myself that sometimes things are too good to be true, in this case the relationship between these two women turned out to be both good and true. Sensitive, warm, and caring, Connie and Todd are cut from the same cloth. Completing the picture was Todd's dad, Tom, who lives in Orange County; both he and his wife Kathy approved of Kari from the outset. So did Todd's cousin Bill, who was instantly captivated.

* * * * *

I had always expected Kari would eventually be ready to live on her own, to cook, to carry groceries up a long flight of stairs, to be in an apartment by herself. I knew very well that Kari II seemed to thrive on challenges. And I trusted my gut feelings about Todd. I had expected good things from him since I'd first read his email.

Still, when Todd and Kari first told me they were ready to move in together, while it was no surprise, it did catch me a little off guard.

As a father, I felt somewhat protective of my daughter and would have preferred that she and Todd at least be engaged before moving in together. In that sense, I was torn. Kari was limited by her ability to find special people to match her unique gifts. Todd, meanwhile, was a father's dream. He cared; he had a present and a future. His life was expanded by Kari and her life by him. No one, I reminded myself, can predict where relationships will go, and this one certainly seemed to be promising.

Gin and I had long discussed Kari's eventual independence. Now, all of a sudden, our daughter was ready to move out and we weren't quite ready to let go. What really made it work for us was Todd's determination to convince Gin and me of how serious he was about Kari. The last thing he wanted was for his presence to have a negative impact on her recovery. Thanks to him, we worked through our concerns quickly and forthrightly. And we all felt a lot better when the two of them located a vacant apartment just nine short blocks away from our house.

On the Thanksgiving weekend, almost a year after they started dating, Todd and Kari moved into their apartment together. From the looks in their eyes, Gin and I concluded the whole affair was destined for nothing short of marriage, anyway. They might as well get a head start.

Shortly before Kari's Web encounter, Kristin, too, found the love of her life in a young man named Scott. Over time, they have become engaged-to-be-engaged. Shortly after the two girls first started dating Scott and Todd, when our cat had kittens, I came up with a plan. Tradition in our house was that I got to do the kitten-naming.

I told Ginger, "I want to name one of them 'Esty, S-T' after Scott and Todd."

"Are you really sure? What happens if one of them breaks up?" Gin asked.

"I don't know. I kind of expect to have these two guys around for a long time. A lot longer than I expect to have the kitten around, anyway." As it turned out, my "father's intuition" was working well.

* * * * *

Kristin's four years in college was in parallel to Kari's recovery. In June 2000, it was time for her to graduate. She had chosen the University of Redlands Johnston Center for her college education. The Johnston Center allows bright, independent students to custom design their college area of emphasis and to largely write their curriculum. The College attracts the creative who are in search of life and its experiences. Graduates often take very long, circuitous paths to their diplomas. The program is very small and very personally oriented. Kristin was remarkably able to take her degree in four years. After her freshman year, complete with its usual trappings of finally and emphatically cutting the remaining cords to the parental units, Kristin told us one night at dinner, "Thanks for how you raised me. I was so much more prepared for the freedom of college." Her thanks were everything to us.

As graduation approached, Kristin called to tell us she needed to have a seconding speech for her graduation. The Johnston Center has a unique graduation to complete their program. Each graduate, about thirty in number, has a few minutes to stand up and talk about life and their experiences at the College. Each is allowed up to two seconding speeches from a professor, friend, or family member who has meant the most to the graduate in his or her college experience. A timekeeper is named and an old brown overstuffed chair is pulled out on the lawn for his comfort. Kristin elected to have Kari and me second her graduation.

For Kari, it was her first public speech since the accident. She was elated to give back a few very aphasic thoughts in support of the sister who had spent much of her high school days in a hospital. The two are so different. It's astounding, the different combinations possible from the same gene pool. For me, I took the podium momentarily to celebrate my other favorite daughter. This one lost her sister and her parents.

Life was not fair to her at a very tender age. This child was able to accept her parents and her sister back into her life when they miraculously reappeared six months later.

* * * * *

Christmas and the dawn of the new millennium came and went. One Sunday after brunch, Todd awkwardly took Ginger and me aside, one at a time.

"You know how much I love your daughter," he began. "I want to know if you have any problems with my asking her to marry me."

"We're thrilled to have you as a part of the family. You've been so great for Kari. When are you going to ask her?" I responded.

"We're going to Santa Barbara this weekend for a romantic getaway. I'll ask her then."

We were so excited in anticipation of the weekend. When they got back on Sunday, we tried to be nonchalant. We didn't see the famous Kari smile and didn't see the diamond sparkle on the hand. Instead of an engagement report, we were told a story about shower drips, room changes, constant rain, and an otherwise not-so-romantic weekend. But Todd had already formulated a back-up plan. Kari, Todd, Kristin, Scott, Ginger, and I were planning to have dinner together to co-celebrate Valentine's Day and Gin's birthday, which was on February 15.

On Valentine's Day 2000, the six of us went to dinner at Nico's. After we finished dessert, Gin and I exchanged Valentine's gifts. Todd had brought in a big box to the dinner, and he now handed it to Kari. Gin and I glanced at each other, in eager anticipation of what was happening.

Kari ripped open the box and saw another wrapped present inside, which turned out to be an audio book she'd wanted:

The Testament by John Grisham. Kari was so happy to see the book she forgot to dig deeper into the box.

"There's more," Todd said.

"Where? Where?" As always, Kari was delighted.

"Keep going."

Kari's fingers probed farther into the box and found another present. It was quite heavy and covered in Christmas wrap.

"What's this?"

"Open it," Todd encouraged.

She unwrapped this second gift, and the writing on the box declared it to be a weather radio.

As Kari stared at the weather radio box, Todd said, "Open it and show it to everyone."

"OK," Kari said, not quite sure what to make of a weather radio.

"There are batteries in the bottom so you can use it right away," he lied.

Kari reached in and pulled out…a tape measure.

"That was just to add some weight to the box," he said. "Keep going."

"Oh. Here's another little box with a note on it," Kari reported in a puzzled tone.

"And…," Todd encouraged again.

"And the note says," Kari studied it carefully, "'I love you today, tomorrow, and forever'….Yes! Yes! *Yes!*"

Kari forgot all about opening the ring box. Instead she jumped up and threw her arms around Todd. He never had a chance to get into the proper position for a proposal.

When Kari finally released him from her grasp, he managed to get down on his knee and, with tears in his eyes, he said, "Kari, I love you more today, tomorrow, and forever. Will you marry me?"

Kari screamed again, "*Yes! Yes! Yes!*" By then tears were coursing down her cheeks.

Everyone in the restaurant burst into spontaneous applause. Kari jumped up and went from table to table, show off her beautiful diamond ring. Not one person who celebrated with us at Nico's will ever forget that Valentine's Day.

I know I won't.

* * * * *

Kari and Todd both wanted an outdoor wedding ceremony, so they set their wedding date for October 2000, hoping to miss the heat and beat the rain. When we added up all the people who would want to attend the wedding, we came up with more than three hundred. Kari and Todd immediately set off to look at potential beach, ocean bluff, and forested wedding sites in southern California that could accommodate that many people.

One afternoon, I offered to take them over to the Virginia Country Club in Long Beach. I had joined the club in May 1999, hoping to renew my interest in golf. Shortly after Kristin was born, while we were living in Mexico, I sold my golf clubs and took up tennis. My reason for doing this was to be able to spend more time with my daughters by exchanging golf, which takes five-plus hours on a weekend, for tennis that can be played in an hour or two. When I sold my clubs, I stated I would take up golf again when my youngest was eighteen. My move to Long Beach was the perfect point for making this long-planned change.

What led me to suggest they consider using Virginia was that the ceremony and reception could be held at a single location, handling any number of guests outdoors and about 325 people in the clubhouse.

What attracted Todd and Kari was a particular spot along the eleventh fairway with a stand of hundred-year-old trees.

Those trees created an enormous canopy over an area of green grass, which is bordered by a lush variety of plants that extend in all directions. It was a natural cathedral, perfect for Kari and Todd. They decided their wedding would be right there.

* * * * *

In March, Kari, Ginger and Kristin headed out on what they all thought would be the beginning of a long search for *the perfect dress*. At the first store, they found an interesting collection of gowns and by the third try-on, were almost certain they had found it. Just to be sure, they checked out a couple more bridal shops. At the second stop, they took a quick look around, shook their heads, and headed right back to the first store. There they bought the wedding gown that had won Kari's heart from the beginning. They ordered the bridesmaids' dresses too, while they were at it.

There is always a certain amount of tension during wedding preparations, because everyone has a different way of wanting to make sure each detail is handled perfectly. But Kari's wedding preparations were relatively tension-free. Most prenuptial pressure is a three-way tug-of-war between the dreams of the bride, the vision of her mother, and the budget of her father. I solved my part of the equation by giving Kari and Gin an unlimited budget. It was a dream come true that we were planning Kari's wedding, and I didn't really care if I spent my last dollar. And as for conflicts between Kari and Gin, they'd been through so much together by then that somehow the wedding plans just didn't seem worthy of bruised feelings.

And so the dresses were bought, the bridesmaids fitted, the flowers picked, the music selected, the menu chosen. Thousands of details had to be attended to so the princess and her prince could bring to life the bedtime stories Gin had told Kari so many times after her return from the hospital.

At the rehearsal dinner held at Lasher's, which had become our new Misto's, I watched the festivities with a sense of wonder. I couldn't help but recall how Kari had dreamed the dream and done the work—courageously—day after day, to make it happen. When it came time for me to give my toast, I rose and spoke from my heart.

"Good evening. I would like to welcome the wedding party and the friends who have joined us for the rehearsal dinner. It's hard to believe that we are so close to the marriage of Todd and Kari. One of Kari's favorite movies is *Pretty Woman*. In the movie Julia Robert's character says, 'I want it all. I want the whole fairytale.'

"Well, Kari and Todd met in the modern-day forest, the Internet. They were destined to meet and destined to walk out of the forest hand and hand. I would like to toast Prince Todd and Princess Kari. May your love be so deep as to survive the days that don't seem like a fairytale and so sweet as to enjoy the countless days where your lives continue to live the wonderful tale."

* * * * *

October 7 dawned pale and overcast, thankfully unmarred by either pelting rain or melting sun. It was a perfect day. The bridesmaids gathered at our house to have their makeup applied and their hair professionally arranged. Along with the bride, they too were treated like royalty.

I sat downstairs at my desk for a part of the morning thinking about the past twenty-five years and particularly, about the last seven. What a matchless journey our family had taken, and Kari could never have walked her path alone. She'd had company, both near and far. More people had reached out to her than we could have possibly foreseen. Whatever else, I knew for a fact that when Kari needed it most, she'd had a close family that refused to look back, but fixed their eyes on the future; an extended family that had loved and prayed and hoped and believed; therapists who had became emotionally connected; nurses and doctors who had given her far more than their jobs required of them.

Maybe she'd even had an assist from On High; maybe her path had been guided all along. In any case, Kari had emerged a true princess, about to marry the prince of her dreams. And, in very different ways, like the characters in so many ancient myths, both of them had been positively transformed as they'd wrestled with their personal struggles.

Before I knew it, my reverie was cut short, and we were on our way to the Virginia Country Club for the wedding. Guests were beginning to arrive; after they parked their cars they were transported to the eleventh fairway canopy in golf carts. With family members around me, I tried to make small talk but was too excited and distracted. *Kari was getting married.* That she was alive was amazing enough; that she was getting married was wonderful beyond belief.

At last I saw her. Her gown was long and strapless with a flowing skirt that swirled around her, as graceful as she was. Delicate silver and pearl beading accentuated her slender figure. She couldn't have been more beautiful. Soon her bridesmaids—sister Kristin; friends Kirsten Stadler and Dana Allen; and relatives Julie, Todd's sister, and Erin, my younger sister's daughter—surrounded her. Like Kari, they wore strapless gowns—theirs in a warm shade of buttercup yellow—with scarves that floated around their shoulders.

Finally, the guests were seated and the music swelled. Two by two, the wedding party marched down the aisle and gathered under the trees, which formed a verdant canopy above them. The ring bearer, Gin's nephew Grayson, found his way across the manicured grass, carefully balancing the pillow that held the rings, with such a look of concentration on his face that his tongue was almost touching his nose

At last, it was our turn. Kari and I began our long walk together. When I'd first seen her that day, Kari had looked a little anxious and worried. But in that moment, Kari was magically changed into the radiant bride she'd always wanted to be. She was aglow with joy and exhilaration. She was too beautiful for words.

I looked out across the crowd at the faces of so many friends, so many family members who love Kari, and helped her along the way. Suddenly, I was back at Daniel Freeman, in the little chapel. Somehow, against all odds, my daughter had lived to fulfill a dream—both hers and mine. I glanced ahead and saw Todd, waiting for Kari at the altar. How many times had Kari and I rehearsed this event, while she was still in a coma and a wheelchair? All at once, my heart was so full my eyes misted over.

I wasn't alone with my tears. I don't think there was one person at the wedding who wasn't weeping by the time we reached the altar. Once there, Kari hugged me, and then turned to Todd, her face alight with happiness.

First, Kari said her vows.

"Todd, I've been looking for you all my life. You are my best friend and the one I want to share my life with. I will love you forever and have faith in you. I will encourage you in everything you do. I will be here to listen to you, to laugh with you, and to hold you. I will work with you as we build our lives together. I will strive every day to make our relationship stronger. You complete my life and soul. I will be your friend, your love, and you partner for all the days of our lives. Will you be my husband?"

Then Todd recited his vows to Kari.

"Kari, you're a dream come true. Words cannot describe the joy and happiness you've brought into my life. I promise to always cherish every moment we have together. I will be there to support you and stand by you always. I will work with you as we build our lives together. Not only will I be your husband today and always but your best friend too. I promise to love you today, tomorrow, and forever. Will you be my wife?

To the formal question, "Do you Todd, take Kari, to have and to hold from this day forward? " Todd surprised us all by almost shouting, "*Absolutely!*"

His response was totally spontaneous and profoundly moving to us all.

Finally the new Mr. and Mrs. were introduced, and there they stood, beaming with delight, beginning their marriage, bound together by more love than most couples ever experience in an entire lifetime of partnership.

The reception allowed all the guests to express their pleasure and to share the memories our family will forever cherish. During the lead-off dance, Gin and I watched Kari and Todd move in unison with "From This Moment On." Like everyone else at the reception, we couldn't help but see the love shining in their eyes. For the traditional father-daughter dance, Kari had chosen the classic recording of Nat King Cole singing "Unforgettable." As she and I danced around the room, Kari held me tightly and the expression on her face said "thank you" in a way that more than made up for all the pain we'd ever shared.

I made my way around the room to greet as many guests as possible and sat down for a few moments with some of the therapists from Daniel Freeman. I thanked each of them from the depths of my heart for the incredibly heroic things they had done to make the occasion possible. More than one responded by saying, "Don't thank me. Thank *you!* Just being here makes all of our work worthwhile."

Kari and Todd danced late into the night. And before the clock struck midnight, the new prince and princess were on their way to the Grand Wailea in Maui for their honeymoon and then…to live happily ever after.

EPILOGUE

On the day after the wedding, the family and the out-of-town guests gathered for a Sunday morning brunch at the house. It was the reverse of a wake. We each had our favorite Kari stories and we told them over and over. Her personality and her spirit had enrolled so many in her recovery. She was the patient but she was really the leader of a successful enterprise.

I couldn't help but share two of my favorite Kari stories. As the previous Christmas was approaching, I casually and carelessly said: "Kari, I'll bet you a million dollars that you can't talk for five minutes without showing any signs of aphasia."

A few days before Christmas Kari said, "Dad, I'm ready for the test." I panicked. She was taking this seriously. Thinking quickly I said: "Tell you what, I'll give you a more realistic $500. If we make it a million dollars that I don't have, I'll have to make you fail. For $500, we'll do it seriously." On Christmas day, Kari spoke easily for the full five minutes, without a hint of aphasia. I spent $500 for another glimpse of the future.

The second story was really about Kristin. When she returned home in the spring of her freshman year, she told her mom she had some good news and some bad news. Both turned out to be bad news to her mom—a nose piercing and a gecko

149

tattoo on her ankle. When I came home, I smiled. Comas are big things. A tattoo and a nose piercing were somehow now not very important.

My sister Lisha asked Gin if she was resentful of all she had given up over the past eight years. Gin thought for a moment and looked out over the water. The sun and water reflected the peacefulness of her mood. "Nobody else in the world could have done what I did. No one was close enough to Kari to give the care that I gave or to give the emotional replenishment that I gave. Look at Kari. Look at that smile. No regrets. I have been rewarded ten times over. No, make that a thousand times over," Gin replied.

Gin reminded us all of a recent event that had major meaning to Kari. The summer before, my extended family had gathered for a reunion at Lake Arrowhead. On the first afternoon, we walked down to the dock to McKenzie's Water Ski School. We had made some advance reservations for the school to teach several members of the family how to ski. They also planned to give a tow to just the more experienced members of the group, including my eighty-one-year-old father. Kari walked down to the dock with Gin and me to confirm our reservation times for the next two days. As usual, Kari got *that* look in her eye. Post-accident, she'd had a lot of difficulty learning that breathing generally occurs above the waterline instead of beneath it! She was becoming water-safe but not comfortably. However, Kari was undaunted by fact; she was driven by conviction. "I want to ski. Can you teach me?" Kari asked as casually as if she were deficit-free.

The next day two ropes were thrown out of the ski boat. Kari was gently nudged into the water with her skis on and supported by a life vest. The instructor moved over next to her and explained, "I'll grab you by your life vest and help support you until you get on top of the water and have your balance comfortably. You ready?"

"Hit it!" And off they went. With the aid of the extra balance point, Kari emerged out to the water and was skiing. Back on the dock the whole family was laughing through their tears. From that day forward, Kari's back, which had been giving her so much pain, was miraculously and dramatically improved. Where in medical school do they teach that the best cure for a chronic bad back resulting from an auto accident is waterskiing?

Three weeks after they returned from Hawaii, Kari and Todd joined Kristin and Scott and Gin and me for dinner at our home. As we were sipping wine, we started talking about the miracle of Kari's recovery, about all the joys and all the pain we'd shared.

While the others talked, my mind replayed the story, scene by scene: The police officer at the door. The emergency room. The hopelessness of the Harbor-UCLA prognosis. The stirrings of response. Trying to reach Kari through music, through telling her stories. I remembered the enormous work of the Freeman rehab team. Of giving Kari the tools to reenter life and to live.

Through it all, I had learned patience and mellowness. Before that, some internal taskmaster had driven my life. I had planned things meticulously and was intensely frustrated when they didn't happen according to my specifications. I had attempted to use my will to control events, in spite of mitigating realities. For obvious reasons, I wasn't always a happy man nor had I always brought happiness to those around me.

The accident had forced me to change my style and my point of view. Maybe it was a gift from Kari. Maybe it was even a gift from God. Nowadays, I wake up almost every day genuinely feeling life is good. When people ask me how I am doing, I never say "fine." I say "super!"

As the six of us continued to talk, all at once Kari said, "If I could go back in time and have the chance to change what happened that night, I wouldn't. So much positive has happened to me and to my family. I made new friends. Dad, you're so much more relaxed about life. And...I met Todd!"

Kristin chimed in. "I agree. I think the accident has been so positive for all of us."

All this was more than a small tribute to our family and to our extended family of friends and therapists. But still...

"Look," I said, shaking my head. "If I could climb into Michael J. Fox's Delorean, be propelled back to Crestridge, and be given the opportunity to stop the U-turn, to prevent the accident and all the pain we've been through from happening, I'm sure I would stop it."

I paused for a moment, glanced at my family, and said, "Or would I?"

Kari and Todd's life continues to be lived forward. In the spring 2001, Kari was accepted as a volunteer (and later as an employee) at the Aquarium of the Pacific in Long Beach. As with so many things, the location choice had special meaning in Kari's life. Todd had arranged to take Kari to the aquarium for their first date. Now, she was returning to the scene of her first date with her first job.

In June 2001, Kari completed her work and graduated from the Acquired Brain Injury program at Coastline Community College. On the day before her ceremony, Kari's primary professor whom she admired enormously, Tracy Goldberg, reviewed her preenrollment cognitive skill results and compared those with her most recent results. Kari improved significantly in almost every category. The next day, Tracy rose to the podium and said, "It gives me great pleasure to announce the outstanding graduate, Kari Crook."

The whole family had transitioned from a small smile of hope engulfed by tears of fear and despair to now laughter coupled with tears of pride, of accomplishment, and of elation. We truly had mastered laughing through the tears.

Kari, age 2, with Luther in Mexico. Unposed.
Natural identical posture.

Kari, age 5, on swing in Michigan.

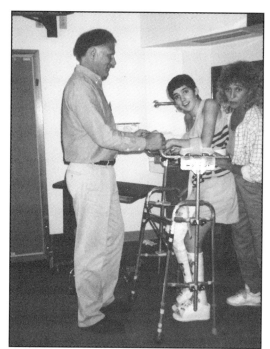

Kari post accident at Daniel Freeman with Luther and
her physical therapist.

Kari at home post accident with friends and sister Kristin (on far right).

Luther and Kari at home.

Kari skiing at Park City for the first time post accident.

Kari running for the first time post accident.

Kari as she appeared on the posting on love@aol.com.

Kari and Todd on their wedding day.

The Nussbaum family, Thanksgiving 2001 (from left to right):
Kristin, Luther, Todd, Dana, Kari, Scott and Ginger.

Reflections for Caregivers: Professional and Family

There are two broad types of medical conditions: degenerative and regenerative. Our experiences and our journey were centered on a regenerative event. Kari basically got better every day. Sometimes it took an extraordinarily observant eye to find the gain, but it was always there. Our experience can speak volumes to those who experience regenerative opportunities.

The human mind seems to establish a baseline for life and its experiences. Our satisfactions, joys, and sorrows come largely from the relationship of our experiences to our expectations. For us to give great care to Kari, we had to reset our expectations.

We knew Kari for eighteen years as a vibrant, sassy, verbal, caring, talented, bright risk-taker. Our expectations were that she would make a significant contribution to the world primarily from her people and verbal abilities. On that warm spring night in 1993 our expectations were shattered. They weren't shattered all at once. Out of intended kindness, the medical profession doles out the bad news over days and sometimes even weeks.

Once the reality of the long-term impact of Kari's accident hit us, we had a choice. We didn't sit around in a family council or even as a husband and wife and consider our alternatives carefully. Perhaps we should have. Over time we evolved our reaction to the overwhelming facts that confronted our old expectations. For us, the only logical place we could go to find emotional comfort was to declare the death of the old Kari. The Kari we knew was dead. We needed to face it. We needed to confront it fully. The comparison of a vegetable to our former daughter could only give us emotional grief.

Out of this need, we evolved the notion of Kari I and Kari II. These terms slowly crept into our vocabulary. It was an easy way of creating two identities with different expectations. It was therapeutic and healthy for us.

Kari II was born on the evening of April 2, 1993. To this day, we celebrate this birth. Regenerative illnesses and accidents provide a basis of joy. As important, they provide a basis for all caregivers to reflect back to the patient extraordinarily positive energy. Sit in a room full of depressed people and try to be happy. Even if they don't say a single word to you, their demeanor sucks energy and life from you—even if you are entirely healthy. Sit in a room of laughing people and try to be sad. Imagine the magnified impact on a person who is fighting for life and fighting to repair massively damaged cells, neural pathways, and organs. For us the most important thing we did was to change our reference set. Kari I and Kari II gave us a framework for becoming positive.

The second lesson of the accident was the power of the written word. From our earliest days, we were encouraged to write down our feelings. In the beginning, Ginger did this on an intermittent basis. As we have scoured our notes, we obviously wished we had written more. However, the lesson to be shared is not about preparation for writing a book. The newsletter, *The Road Back*, was our way of keeping a group of friends who were invested in Kari's recovery informed without having to spend endless hours on the phone rehashing the same stories. When Gin and I would sit down to write the notes for *The Road Back*, we would almost invariably enter the session pessimistically. In spite of our day-to-day optimism, somehow the task of writing about progress intimidated us. We would enter the conversation each believing that this month we didn't have enough material to write an optimistic newsletter. Within minutes after starting our conversation, we were reinforced that Kari had made heroic progress. With our constant involvement we lost perspective. The writing allowed us to be broad and to be reflective. Kari was indeed making progress.

Lesson three is about spirituality. Professional caregivers generally give medicine but not hope and certainly not life. Professionals restore the cell but not the soul. Family caregivers know their patient. They have the tools to give beyond medicine. Our good friends are Christian Scientists. Their belief in God and His gifts are unshakable. Our belief that God is in each of us and our collective healing power is now equally unshakable. Whatever your beliefs, give until it hurts and then give a bit more.

Lesson four is about understanding the patient. For professional caregivers this is incredibly tough. We encountered four groups of caregivers. The elite were able to feel as Kari feels. The best sensed what Kari's body was willing to give. They coaxed that next level of range or next speech pattern out of her. They were able to get in synch with her body and its progress on its journey to recovery. They were able to relax her defenses sometimes by a personal relationship or kind words or humor. Once the defenses were relaxed, it inevitably meant a major leap forward in recovery. The second group of therapists was mechanically excellent and were able to relate personally with Kari. They were able to make considerable progress in working with her. While she consistently and constantly improved under their care, they were never able to experience the significant breakthroughs the elite brought about. The third group had great technical skills but had no patient relationship skills. It is as though they took literally the professional training maxim, "Don't become emotionally involved with your patients." Kari needed a personal relationship of even a modest sort for her body to relax and allow another human being to manipulate her joints beyond their comfort level. The final group was fortunately a very small minority for us. These therapists brought their lives and their hostilities to the workplace. The pain of ranging seemed to satisfy needs from their private lives. To be elite, sense the patient's body while entertaining and distracting the mind.

Lesson five is about teaching. To both professional and family caregivers we would observe the need to educate the family and the patient. We learned so much from the physicians, nurses, and therapists. We were inquisitive. We learned every chance we could by watching the different therapists and asking them about what they were doing. When we could, we read as many articles on brain injury and brain injury rehab as our numbed minds could absorb. We knew Kari but we didn't have the benefit of the years of training in the specialty disciplines that surrounded us in the hospital and in the rehab facility. We were voracious learners.

One day Jackie Devries said, "The two of you are the perfect complements. Luther, you are the motivator. Ginger, you are the comforter." Roles are very necessary. The key males in Kari's life were her motivators: Adrian, me, and finally Todd. Ginger is so supportive, caring, and comforting. Because we each had roles, I could push Kari. I could challenger her. When tears came, Ginger could feel as Kari felt and give her the emotional uplift she craved.

In illness, as in health, there are introverts and extroverts. A simple definition of an introvert is that introverts recharge alone by themselves. After a tough day, they want to get away from people. Extroverts are the reverse. Extroverts want company. They thrive on the energy derived from being with friends. Illness exacerbates these natural tendencies. For Kari, a strong extrovert, she couldn't get enough interaction with people. Her reaction is unique to her. Know your family member; know your patient.

From the earliest days, we decided we wanted Kari back into life. Given the breakdown in Kari's communication systems for two-and-a-half months, we were unable to talk with her about her feelings. We had to guess. I imagined we were in a tug of war with the next life. Whether heaven or hell was pulling, I'll leave to others. To get Kari back to this life and then to push her brain to recover as far and as fast as possible, we elected to engage Kari in life. Our first outings were not as much about going home as they were out into the community. We regularly went to theme parks, shopping malls, and restaurants. Whenever we could manage it we put Kari on an airplane to expose her to new experiences and new situations. Someone said early on, "If Kari learns to walk better she will talk better. All functions are interrelated in the brain." For us this was a core thought. After every trip, we could notice measurable improvements in Kari's functional ability. Exposing her to new situations and new events was one of her most important therapies.

Kari obviously found great opportunity in this observation. She would give us *that* look and say, "Dad, I think I need more therapy. How about a trip to Hawaii?"

We believe in the healing power of personal contact. Our days at Harbor-UCLA were schizophrenic. We wanted so much to give Kari more and more contact. We were watching the ICP monitor so much we couldn't accomplish all that we wanted. When we arrived at Daniel Freeman we found a much more relaxed and supportive atmosphere, appropriate to her improving condition. Kari was out of the most immediate danger and they allowed us and her friends to climb into bed with her for wonderful hug sessions. The power of human contact is astounding.

Finally, we have been blessed to have personal financial resources. We were also blessed that our insurance carrier went the distance with us. While there were battles and tense moments, Kari received the care she needed. Because of this, both Ginger and I were able to spend many hours at the hospital in the role of family caregivers. We were able to observe Kari during therapy and to see things the therapists didn't see. We were able to sense things from knowing our daughter better than they ever could. During the early weeks we were probably too willing to trust the professionals. The instinct that comes from knowing the patient is a powerful assist in recovery. Whatever the hours your personal situation can give, spend them. Spend them in an observing, caregiving mode.

ACKNOWLEDGMENTS

Without the paramedic team's incredibly fast response that April night, Kari would never have made it out of a vegetative state. The team, headed by Battalion Chief Bob Belliveau from Fire Station #106 in Rancho Palos Verdes, extricated Kari from the Previa van using the Jaws of Life and rushed her to the trauma center at Harbor-UCLA. The surgical team led by Dr. Duncan McBride gave her a new lease on life. The intensive care nurses, whose names have been lost in our history, gave superb care to the vegetative Kari. Our hearts have a special place for a young occupational therapist known only to us as Janie who dedicated hours she didn't have to teach us how to "range" our daughter and to preserve her from the ravages of tone. Similarly, the young, infectious disease specialist practiced great medicine coupled with a deep caring for our daughter.

Daniel Freeman was a magical place for us. Kari entered as a vegetable and emerged again as a young lady. The physicians, therapists, nurses, and staff all contributed so incredibly to her recovery. With the risk of omitting many who cared, I would like to recognize five who made all-star contributions. Lynn Butler was Kari's soul mate from the beginning. Lynn's intuition about and connection with Kari made a huge difference in her recovery. Jackie Devrees was a brilliant occupational therapist, always working patiently and persistently with Kari. Waleed A'boudi was Barishnikov. His sessions with Kari were ballet. Herlene MccLees said Kari would never run again and then preceded to coax every bit of range that was available from Kari's legs, which of course was enough for her to run. Colleen Byrne worked endless hours on Kari's hands adding flexibility and functionality. As with so many, Colleen became a friend as well as a therapist for Kari.

The American healthcare system is in the throes of real turmoil. I work in the industry and understand its problems from a close perspective. However, nothing demonstrates the success of the system like Kari's heroic recovery. It is part medicine and in part the remarkable personal commitment of the healthcare professionals.

When I entertained the task of writing this book, a close friend, Al Nagy, suggested I use a ghostwriter. I had talked too long about the project and one business crisis after another postponed my serious commitment to writing. As always, Al had a person to suggest, Lela Gilbert. Lela asked me to go deep into my emotions to express how I felt along this eight-year journey. Her gift for telling stories and her easy way of communicating complex issues shows in the finished manuscript.

My mental health was assisted by a group of friends who are part of my Young President's Group forum. To lose a daughter is to lose a big part of life. To reassemble life, and turn this event into a birth and a new life took incredible emotional commitment. Al Nagy, Paul Mikos, Steve Olson, Steve Hauck, Ty Bobit, Pete Grande, Jay Haskell, Kris Friedrich, Sam King, Spike Irwin, and Jim Slavik provided me with the support structure I needed to make it through the darkest hours. Another YPOer, Lou Kwiker, had a knack of showing up at the right time at the hospital to bring another smile and dose of optimism.

No list would be complete without mentioning the incredible contribution of Ken and Mary Ellen Crow. Behind the scenes they were the rock. They put their lives on hold to support us and to make things happen so that we could focus all of our efforts on Kari's recovery. Similarly, Mary Ritter, the mother of one of Kari's ex-boyfriends, spent hours at the hospital coaxing Kari back to health and supporting us.

We didn't cook a meal for weeks after the accident thanks to Las Madrecitas, the Palos Verdes Junior League, P.E.O. and other friends. What incredibly giving people.

Kari's high school friends made the first year tolerable. Kari was the ringleader of the group and had given so much to so many. Their daily trips to the rehab center continued to give Kari the human contact that motivated her recovery. A special thanks goes to Adrian Lengsfeld, her boyfriend before the accident. Adrian found ways to encourage and motivate Kari beyond the reach of any of the rest of us.

During Kari's long recovery two individuals lived with us at the house to serve as Kari's companion and driver. Each, ultimately, became a member of the family and a close friend of Kari's. Dana Allen and Matthew Aguinaga invested so incredibly in her long road back.

Within the first year after Kari left Daniel Freeman, we were knocking on the door of Santa Monica College to get her admitted into the Acquired Brain Injury Reentry Program. Sandy Burnett and Lee Pazutti were saints in admitting someone way too early in her recovery cycle, but it gave Kari the human contact she needed to stay motivated. Several years later, Coastline Community College and Tracy Goldberg have given Kari the tools, skills, and confidence to return to the workaday world. A special thanks goes to the wonderful staff headed by Warren Iliff at the Aquarium of the Pacific in Long Beach where Kari was given her first work experience as a volunteer, and is now an employee.

There are three more healthcare professionals who stand out in our journey. Steve Reischl picked up where Herlene left off and continued to work with Kari smoothing out her gait and extending her range. Jim Hawley and Diana Fessler have helped Kari learn how to extend her vision to cope with her blind spots down and to the right.

My assistant, Julee McCarthy, helped enormously in the rewrites of the manuscript, in the long search for an agent and publisher, and in the final checking of names and facts.

At the end of the day, it was my awesome family that really came through. Jody, thanks for dropping everything to come to our aid and to be a temporary mom for Kristin. My immediate family, Leo, Janet, Felicity, and Margaret, lived far and wide but contributed emotion, energy, wisdom, and support. Todd, what a miracle you are in our lives. Kristin, you did so much more over the years for your sister than you'll ever realize. Gin, you are my soul mate and I thank you for all that you are.

Luther Nussbaum
Long Beach, California
Jim455@aol.com
June 25, 2001